The Chilli Pepper club

Published in 2025 by Turn Fire Press
First edition

Editor: Miriam Tobin
Copy editor: Laura Hayes
Cover design and typesetting: Oliver Hutton

sallyjturner.com

The Chilli Pepper club

Sally Turner

Turn Fire Press 2025

Author's note

The personal experiences recounted in this memoir are based on my diaries written at the time the events occurred and my memories in retrospect. As such, they are subjective accounts of what took place.

To protect the privacy of others, names and other identifying details, such as ages and locations, have been changed unless stated otherwise.

No part of this book constitutes medical advice. Always consult a specialist medical doctor for diagnosis and treatment.

Contents

1

Cherry bomb

Out across the bay the sun had set in a blaze of orange, and a light breeze was rustling the coconut palms. We had been walking barefoot along the shore and, as darkness fell, we tumbled through the dunes, dancing on the sand.

I had met Simon just four weeks ago at an after-show party at Kensington Roof Gardens, and we had been loved up ever since. Now, he had flown me out to join him in Antigua where he was shooting a video promo, and I was high on lust and sunshine. Inside a secluded beach house, we lay entwined beneath the cool white sheets of a vast mahogany bed, and he kissed me again. He tasted of champagne and strawberries, and I could smell the ocean on his skin. Slowly, I began to move my body against his, and the desire began to build until…

Jesus, Madonna and Shakin' freakin' Stevens!? I sat bolt upright in my creaky single bed at home in Surrey. My school-night fantasy had culminated in an intense pulsating wave that crashed through me like a lightning bolt.

Leaning over, I clicked on the bedside light, illuminating a wall plastered from floor to ceiling with Duran Duran posters; Simon, John, Nick, Roger and Andy were grinning down at me like an assortment of foiled-wrapped Quality Street in their shiny Anthony Price suits. For the past few weeks – courtesy of a vivid imagination – I had been having a whirlwind fling with the band's singer Simon Le Bon. We had been papped at a host of A-list parties, he had written songs for me, and now…I was in a hormonally charged state of shock. What the hell had just happened? Had I tweaked something I shouldn't have? Was this a muscle spasm or a jangled nerve? My brain was frantically searching the archives for a frame of reference. I was thirteen, and all I could come up with was that it had felt like climbing the tracks on a rollercoaster and then dropping into a bend – shocking, terrifying and thrilling, all at once.

Over the next couple of weeks it slowly began to dawn on me – I'd had an *orgasm*. Holy shit, an orgasm. I was vaguely familiar with the term, but hadn't really known what it meant until now. It was 1982, there was no internet or mobile phone network and only three TV channels. What little I knew of sex I had gleaned from reading my friend's *Jackie* magazines and from the brief 'facts of life' talk my mother had given me a couple of years earlier. We had also been taught the basics in biology lessons at my girls-only high school, but although I was familiar with the mechanics of sex nothing had prepared me for the explosive thrill.

I began to experiment and ditched Simon for the band's bassist John Taylor. I even allowed myself imagined liaisons with mere mortals – the bloke who worked in Our Price and my friend's ultra-cool elder brother. Sexual fantasy and imagined promiscuity had a lot going for it; sex was 10 per cent perspiration, 90 per cent inspiration. It was exciting, safe and secret, though I did feel an occasional twinge of guilt at what I was getting up to. Like cake, chips, and chocolate, surely something that could make me feel this good must be bad in some way? Now and again the God of school assemblies would haunt me beneath my polycotton sheets, and I would offer up a half-hearted prayer of dispensation:

"Dear God. Please forgive me if doing this is not okay. And please bless my family and friends and all the starving people in Africa. Amen."

My mother's words also hung in the air with pre-Febreze persistence. She had told me sex should be saved for marriage and I had this nagging feeling that, at the very least, there should be someone else in the room rather than just plastered across the wall.

At school we would discuss periods, boys and disco smooching, but nobody ever admitted to masturbation. Though a couple of months later, in my dentist's waiting room, I read an article in an old *She* magazine that eased my conscience. Apparently sexual fantasy and DIY sex were normal, even recommended. I celebrated by working my way through a choice selection of Top 40 stars and Hollywood idols. A couple of years later, I even bopped Kevin Bacon's character in teen flick *Footloose*. We busted some dance moves at his high-school prom before he seduced me behind a tractor in a Mid-West farm scape.

My only regret was that I'd had my first bite at the cherry with a pop pin-up instead of waiting for hot Aussie rock god Michael Hutchence of INXS. Watching him breathless and entangled with Paula Yates on Channel 4's *Big Breakfast* bed was like televisual poppers, but at least I was ready when he showed up.

Channelling this sexual energy through the safe, smiling filter of pop fantasy diluted its intensity, but instinctively I knew I had tapped into something that ran far deeper, of which school-night imaginings were just the visible tip. I felt the gravitational pull of something wild and primal; a shadowland was beckoning, at its centre a core of molten energy and longing.

I had encountered this potent life force before in other guises. It had flowed along with the blood, scarlet on white cotton, six months before I turned thirteen. When I told my mother my period had arrived, she looked teary-eyed. I comforted her as she mumbled "I've lost my little girl". Then she apologised and handed me a retro-style sanitary towel that felt like a plank of wood between my legs. The blood smelt pungent and metallic, and the strangeness of it all took some getting used to – my mother's ambivalent reaction, the cramps, and the bulky pads that couldn't be trusted to keep my awkward secret. But slowly, as the blood arrived every month, cyclical like a wheel turning, I sensed the power and energy of its rhythm. I felt my body awakening, eager to start a journey. It had plans it wanted me to roll with, and this monthly rush of hormonal energy was fuel in the engine.

Long before the onset of puberty, in the innocent sensuality of childhood, I had felt this same life-blood pulse in the earth as I lay against an oak tree, fancying I could hear it breathing and growing. It was in the rich sensory hit of the ripened blackberries we had collected and stewed to make jelly, straining through white muslin over the bath; in the feel of my warm pet rabbit's speckled fur and beating heart, and in the earthy magic of timeless fairy tales: "Bite into the apple", "Spin the wheel", "Come in, my pretty".

It all came from the same source, this energy that throbbed through the living. Sometimes it was an intangible background hum in the woods, on the wind, in the silence; at other times it was visceral and intensely felt through blood, gnarled tree trunks, soil and sex. Was this force the 'God' I had heard about in church and school assemblies? I didn't think so. It felt more animate than ethereal; it was difficult to fully comprehend or articulate. And now, in my teens, it emerged once more in a new chameleon-like guise. This time it had a groove on like a Madonna pop video, but beneath the '80s electronica was the throbbing bass beat of a pagan stomp. It was something to be felt rather than described; something I couldn't quite put my finger on. Well, not metaphorically anyway; in a more literal sense I was becoming quite the expert at night under the covers. And as I surfaced from beneath the duvet into a world spinning with 12-inch remixes and boys' school parties, I soon graduated from imagined liaisons to real-world dancefloor snogging and a bit of light groping.

I was eager for further amorous encounters, but my enthusiasm was tapered with self-consciousness; I loved my legs but loathed my crooked teeth and my A-cup boobs. I had planned on inheriting the gene for my mother's ample bosom, but instead I was gifted my grandmother's skinny physique. I had also inherited my parents' tendency toward perfectionism, anxiety and overthinking which, mercifully, was tempered with their quick wit and a creative streak. Aged fourteen, I was a potent cocktail of hand-me-down combustibles and the fuse was about to be lit. I wanted to blaze through life and dazzle like a firework extravaganza, but it was equally possible I would implode like a badly-planned sixties tower block – or worse, just fizzle unnoticed by the wayside. Only time would tell, and as I plodded on through rocky teenage terrain the weight of my potential rubbed me raw like an unwieldy backpack.

My world was one of constant comparisons, and in the cloakroom at school we compared bra size, zit outbreaks and tampon absorbency, but we rarely discussed the geography of what lay beneath our navy A-line skirts. My "nether regions" – to coin the phrase my mother used – were a secret source of pleasure and occasional guilt, but otherwise devoid of sensation and excluded from conversation. I had no idea they were about to take centre stage in an epic drama, but on a hot July day in 1984, a month after my fifteenth birthday, I woke up to Scene One.

2

Molten underworld

Scene One: Sore throat, swollen glands, sharp stabbing pain in lower back.

My GP ran some tests and diagnosed a kidney infection and a "glandular-fever-related virus". A two-week course of antibiotics should sort out the kidney infection he said, and my body would fight off the virus; I just needed to rest. Sure enough, within a few days the lower back pain disappeared, but another symptom had taken its place: a vaginal discharge which caused localised soreness, burning and itching. I had never experienced anything like this before, so I told myself it must be something to do with the kidney infection and that it would clear up in a few days, but the discomfort persisted.

Unbeknown to me, these symptoms would mark the beginning of a seismic shift. The powerful molten underworld I had sensed within was beginning to erupt, not as erotic pleasure but as burning pain, and it was about to change the landscape of my life entirely.

Two weeks later, I chanced upon an item about vaginal thrush in the problem pages of teen magazine *Mizz*. The symptoms described were familiar; the agony aunt explained that thrush was a yeast infection, an overgrowth of the fungal yeast candida albicans, and could occur after taking a course of antibiotics which often upset the vagina's delicate microflora.

Candida is a naturally occurring fungal yeast that lives in the gut, bowel, vagina and mouth. It usually causes no problem, but a candidiasis infection can develop if conditions change which encourage the yeast to multiply. Broad-spectrum oral antibiotics are a common trigger as they kill microbes throughout the body, including the 'good' organisms which keep the 'bad' ones in check.

Antibiotics can also wreak havoc on the gut. Around 70 to 80 per cent of our immune system cells are located here and, for some people, changes to the gut microbiome can have a detrimental effect on systemic immunity[1], and play a part in the development of conditions such as depression[2] and Parkinson's disease[3]. Swallowing probiotic capsules does not always restore microbes to previous healthy levels. One study found that six months after taking broad-spectrum antibiotics, some participants only recovered about 63 per cent of the bacterial species they had before the treatment and they had also lost many of the 'friendly' species that maintain gut health[4].

Along with antibiotics, other things that can disrupt the vaginal microflora include hormonal fluctuations, dietary and immune system changes, sexual activity, and some brands of sexual lubricant, wash creams and soaps. A healthy vagina has a low pH level of between 3.8 and 4.2. This is fairly acidic which encourages healthy microbes and impedes the growth of harmful bacteria and yeasts. However, when the pH level is disrupted – for example by menstruation, over-washing, or contact with semen or saliva – conditions such as thrush or bacterial vaginosis may develop, causing uncomfortable symptoms. Around 30 to 50 per cent of women will have at least one vaginal thrush infection during their lifetime, and the probability of developing recurrent vulvovaginal candidiasis after an initial infection is around 25 per cent by the age of fifty years[5].

I went to see the female GP at my local surgery. She took a vaginal swab which came back positive for thrush and handed me a prescription for a four-day course of antifungal vaginal pessaries. They looked like miniature missiles and had an almost fluorescent yellow glow. The discharge and itching disappeared within 48 hours of launching them, but I continued to feel an ongoing burning sensation and a sharp pain around the vaginal entrance when I attempted to insert tampons during my period. I tried to forget about it as I had more pressing health concerns to contend with; the kidney pain might have disappeared but I still had a sore throat and swollen glands, and I had begun to ache all over. I felt faint simply walking a few metres from my bedroom to the bathroom, and travelling a short distance in a car or chatting to a friend left me utterly exhausted.

I was still getting over the virus, said my family GP. My immune system would soon fight it off and in the meantime I should push on with things and go back to school in September.

"You're a fighter, aren't you? You mustn't give in to this," he said with a smile and a fist pump.

And so recovery became about fighting my body, mind over matter.

I dragged myself back to school, determined to beat the symptoms, but most days I would have to be driven home at lunchtime with crushing fatigue, aching muscles and a blinding headache. It was post-viral malaise, said the GP, and in time my immune system would bounce back, but weeks turned into months and my symptoms worsened.

My O-level exam year was a write-off and as for parties, boys and snogging, I would turn up prepped with lashings of black mascara, raring to go, only to be struck dumb by fatigue and 'brain fog' and have to be picked up mid-evening, in humiliating fashion, by my parents. They did their best to keep my spirits up, along with my brother, but none of us really understood how to handle this consuming exhaustion that would regularly floor me like a bowling pin.

Dad was a headteacher and alongside teaching he had spent years as an actor in repertory theatre. He was in his mid-forties by the time I was born, and with his swathe of grey hair and bronzed skin he had the air of an aging matinee idol. As head of the junior school I had attended (from the age of five until eight) he was king of my world. I would watch him on stage every morning in assembly along with a rapt audience of staff and children as he moved deftly between roles, from authority figure to children's entertainer. After school I would have my run of the kingdom through empty classrooms, across the playground and out into the surrounding woods and churchyard, my head spinning with the fairy tales and magic of tattered Ladybird books. He would often hoist me aloft onto his shoulders, and safe on top of the world I would peer into trees and hedgerows looking for birds' nests. He smelt of hair tonic and the promise of summer as I reached over his head to touch the warm speckled eggs of a robin.

Mum taught music at the school and was always busy baking, sewing and making miraculous things out of coloured cardboard and bits of fabric. When she did stop to sit down it was usually to play the piano or to use the sewing machine. At sixteen – after I had dumped

Duran Duran for the indie genius of Julian Cope – she would run old men's paisley pyjamas through the sewing machine (my prized jumble sale finds) and transform them into 'psychedelic' leggings and shirts that I accessorised with strings of beads, knock-off Ray-Bans and plenty of attitude. She was my mother, but also an oversharing friend, comedy partner and symbiotic emotional twin. Whatever she felt I felt – good, bad, or ugly, in the pit of my stomach – as if we were still attached by some energetic umbilical cord.

The summer I fell ill, I had also fallen head over heels for Ozzy, the cool and aloof rich kid who lived in a sprawling old mansion at the posh end of the village. On the rare occasions he did cross my path I was struck dumb with longing so, as a calling card, Mum and I wrote a comedy skit about him based on Michael Jackson's 'Thriller' rap, which Dad voiced (in the style of actor Vincent Price), my best friend enhanced with sound effects, and my brother delivered to his door. It was one of numerous early adventures in 'social media' – armed with '80s pop, a ghetto blaster and a bumper pack of Maxell cassette tapes, we were a creative production hub. The cassette delivery inspired him to cycle over with an invite to his exclusive birthday party at the mansion. When I answered the front door and found him leaning nonchalantly against the door frame I could barely breathe. Somehow I kept my cool, and I had high hopes for the party, but my hopes were soon crushed. I passed out ill way before the stroke of midnight like a half-baked Cinderella, and with toe-curling embarrassment I had to ask his mum if I could call my parents to come and pick me up.

Family life continued to tick over with creative aplomb,

Sunday roasts and magnificent puddings, but beneath the surface we were caught by an undercurrent of middle -class angst. My parents put on a convincing show of cheeriness for public consumption, but off-duty it was often a different story. Mum would find it difficult to regulate her ever-changing feelings and Dad would head for the vegetable patch down the garden under a dark cloud – and disappear emotionally for days or weeks at a time. Love, anger, pain and regret often hung in the air unspoken as we each held on tightly to turbulent emotions. Sometimes, we would hurl them at each other with awkward abandon, but generally they were kept on the back burner, simmering with the lid on until they boiled over once again.

Underlying tensions and my apparent inability to "fight back" and "think" myself well were knocking a dent into my self-esteem; I had exams to work for and boys to impress, but I was failing on all fronts. My body was letting me down and I was beating myself up about it. On top of all this I was aware that something was still seriously amiss down under; my vagina was often sore and uncomfortable and tampons had become even more painful to insert. (Or to be more precise, my *vulva* was often sore and uncomfortable – more on the ins and outs of being genitally PC in a later chapter.)

I went back to see the female GP who didn't bother to examine me again as my initial swab had tested positive for thrush. Instead, she handed me a prescription for more antifungal pessaries along with a leaflet on how to keep vaginal thrush at bay. I followed the advice; I wore cotton knickers and avoided tights, jeans and bubble baths. I smeared myself with 'live' yoghurt (which is full of lactobacilli cultures) to replenish the 'good' bacteria, and smelt like a rancid bowl of muesli, but still the symptoms persisted. Skin-tight 'drainpipe' jeans were an '80s must-have, and everywhere I looked I saw girls swanning around in them taunting me with their vulval resilience.

Over the next two years, I tried just about every brand of topical antifungal on the market – pessaries, coated tampons, iodine douches, creams in applicator tubes – an arsenal of neatly-packaged chemical weaponry. Nothing helped. The discharge had disappeared, but I was still sore and uncomfortable. I also went to see a gynaecologist at the local hospital who gave me some antibacterial cream to try, but that didn't help either.

Six months later I travelled up to London for an appointment with one of Harley Street's "top people" – a private gynaecologist who had been recommended by our family GP. He didn't even examine me; he just gave my medical notes a cursory glance and prescribed six weeks' worth of antifungal pessaries, one per night.

"Chronic thrush can be difficult to treat," he said. "We need to hit it hard over an extended period."

I wanted to hit *him* hard over an extended period, but instead I did what he told me. After all, he was a top Harley Street gynaecologist and I was a seventeen-year-old girl with no internet to consult for a second opinion. But the missile bombardment didn't work. If anything, it aggravated the soreness.

Thankfully, my general health was improving, slowly. After struggling on for over a year with crushing fatigue, I had been unable to manage the schoolwork required to complete my O-levels and passed only four of the 11 subjects I was studying. But over the summer holidays, I managed to recover enough to study for my A-levels.

Two years later, reports of myalgic encephalomyelitis (ME) – or 'Yuppie Flu' as it was referred to in the '80s – began appearing in the media, and I realised the persistent fatigue and flu-like symptoms I'd had were likely down to this.

The day before I turned seventeen, I met my first boyfriend Dylan at a friend's party. He was a couple of years older than me and had a local job as he hadn't gone off to college. Thanks to him my ailing vulva became more than just a source of anxiety and upset. Dylan was gentle and adoring with indie hair and just the right amount of teenage grit and rebellion to keep it interesting – for 18 months anyway. Plus, he was a member of a local poetry collective, the cool-in-my-eyes Winterhill Poets, and could play the guitar riff to Julian Cope's 'Sunspots'. He knew my vulva had issues, but was patient and supportive. On Friday nights we would trade thrills in his single bed while his mum cooked us frozen pizza and oven chips in the kitchen below, and then get it on in deserted carriages on last trains home from music gigs. We never went 'all the way' – I was waiting for 'The One', whatever that meant – but we had plenty of hands-on fun. At times I would experience flare-ups of generalised vulval soreness, but most of the time the burning pain was centred around the vestibule (the entrance to the vagina) so non-penetrative sex was still on the table, and underneath it at house parties.

Real-world adventures in Dylan's bedroom knocked the socks off my solo pop fantasies. Yes, reality sucked when the pain flared up, but it rocked when I was tuned into the pleasure vibe in Dylan's box-room haven. However, I would soon be leaving for college in London and life was about to take a different turn. As I packed my bags and headed for the 'Capital of Cool' it felt a long way from Winterhill and my imaginary sexploits in Antigua. And along with my belongings, I carried with me the weight of my plummeting self-esteem and the growing tension between the pain and pleasure of my sexuality.

3

Poker face

Student HQ for the next three years was in London's West End. The PCL campus on Riding House Street was a stone's throw from the BBC's Broadcasting House and the ITN/Channel 4 studios, and close to the buzzing backstreets of Soho – home to a myriad of independent production companies. PCL, aka the Polytechnic of Central London, was one of the few academic institutions in the UK during the '80s that offered a vocational media degree (before 'meedya studies' was vilified as Mickey Mouse) and spawned the pop culture wit'n'grit of writers Jon Ronson and Charlie Brooker. It later became the University of Westminster – a pimped up poly with a new moniker. I was studying a combo of print journalism, radio and video production, with some socio-cultural theory thrown in by a pithy middle-aged lecturer in brown cords to give it some academic oomph.

My relationship with Dylan didn't survive more than a term of college. He was still living at home, and I was caught up in a whirl of new faces and ideas and wanted to spread my wings. I was living a typical undergrad existence, though something crucial was missing – sex. Friends bragged and joked about their sexual exploits, and I laughed in all the right places, but I was holding on tightly to my embarrassing secret. Public and home internet access was still years away, but I scoured the library for everything I could find on sexual health; if the doctors couldn't fix me I would have to do it myself. I read up on the alternative medicine approach – herb poultices, lemon and vinegar douches, acidophilus capsules. I went to see a homeopath and went on an anti-candida diet that involved cutting out yeast and refined sugar. I even made the ultimate student sacrifice and gave up wine and cider in favour of whisky, as I had read that distilled alcohol was less of an irritant. (I had bladder symptoms now too and often experienced twinges of bladder pain and burning, yet tests proved negative for bacterial infection.) But nothing I tried had any obvious healing effect.

Despite recurrent symptoms of pain and soreness, my desire still burned strong and I wanted to get my rocks off with someone new, but I felt vulnerable in this sexually-charged environment where full-on shagging was the expected norm. I was a virgin with a faulty vagina and for 18 months, while I eyed up the possibilities, an unconscious part of me sent out signals that said "I'm damaged goods, leave me on the shelf".

But then, one day in June, Stuart knocked at the front door of our student digs in Turnpike Lane. The elder brother of a recently arrived housemate, he was studying for his finals in philosophy and would ramble on about existentialism while we smoked his stash of dope. I was impressed that he thought about the bigger picture and lent me books by French novelists I had never heard of – Flaubert and Zola. Apparently, he hadn't picked up my ailing vagina vibes and he asked me out.

Stuart lived in the basement of an old house in Holland Park, a world away from our student 'ghetto' in Haringey.

He rented it from a musician who had been at the forefront of punk in the '70s, which lent it an air of decadent cool even though it was in a state of total disrepair. He was into The Doors and had a pseudo-Jim-Morrison thing going on, plus he cooked sophisticated pasta using a recipe, a step up from the standard tinned tuna, tomatoes and mushy rigatoni our household lived on. I'm going to sleep with him, I thought. Perhaps he wasn't 'The One', but I felt comfortable enough with him to go for it. I was almost twenty and my virginity had begun to feel like a millstone around my neck. 'Real' sex felt like something I should have done by now, and I was keen to find out what all the fuss was about. I was still experiencing regular bouts of soreness and burning, but perhaps in the heat of passion ecstasy would eclipse the pain.

I told Stuart it was my first time, and he did all the right things; he made sure I was relaxed and turned on and we used a condom, but as he tried to enter me the pain was excruciating. Eventually, he managed to ease his way in, but the pain sharpened, and I had to ask him to stop.

"Oh well," he said nonchalantly, "technically you can say you're not a virgin anymore."

We put it down to first-time discomfort and decided to give it another go in a couple of days.

Forty-eight hours later I was back in his bed determined to try again. We took things slowly but still it was agony. Through gritted teeth I managed to cope with a couple of thrusts but had to beg him to stop. It felt as though someone was plunging a red-hot poker into me. Hot tears began to roll down my cheeks. I had hoped that having 'real' sex would liberate me from vagina angst and make me feel like a 'real' woman at last. Instead, I felt more insecure than ever.

Stuart did his best to comfort me. "Perhaps we need to try a different position," he ventured the next morning, tossing a tattered paperback in my direction. "Have a look at this and see if there's anything you fancy trying out later."

Toast in hand, he grabbed his wallet and dashed off to his temp job. I picked up the book. It was a faded '70s copy of *The Joy of Sex*. Between its covers a hirsute couple was depicted exploring sex in all its diversity. The bloke looked like a caveman from a junior-school textbook, and his partner had a bush in need of some serious topiary. Okay, my own bikini line wasn't exactly immaculately trimmed – it was less 'Brazilian' landing-strip, more 'Amazonian rainforest' – but I wanted my sexual imagery to at least feel relevant to the impending '90s, rather than circa 1973, or the Neolithic era.

The retro sex illustrated in Stuart's dog-eared book seemed more mechanical than erotic. I flicked through the pages looking for an inspired posture that might make for a comfortable shag, but nothing I saw particularly whetted my appetite. I wanted to feel excited by this feast of sexual variety, but instead I felt apprehensive and more insecure than ever. Suddenly it wasn't enough just to have pain-free sex and enthusiasm alone would not suffice. To be good in bed I would have to perfect a sexual repertoire of weird and wonderful techniques and contortions.

We experimented with a couple of different positions and tried using a pH-balanced lubricant and hypoallergenic condoms, but the pain and the burning were still intolerable. Desperate, I downed a considerable amount of Glenfiddich and was numb enough to endure a couple of minutes of thrusting. I was too comatose to feel any pleasure either, but I was having sex and that was all that mattered. I've done it, I thought, but it was a hollow victory. When I awoke from my whisky-induced stupor the next morning I was in agony. It felt as if someone had taken a blowtorch to my vulva. I dragged myself to Stuart's bathroom armed with a travel-sized pack of self-help potions and gently applied aqueous cream and doused myself with cold water, but the fire raged on, for five whole days. The pain was so intense I could barely function or focus.

I didn't know where to turn. I had seen two eminent gynaecologists and tried numerous natural remedies. Remarkably, my symptoms hadn't dampened my desire; I still enjoyed the great orgasms I had with Stuart through mutual masturbation. But whereas with Dylan this had been an end in itself it was now relegated to foreplay – an appetiser for an entrée I couldn't provide. I would have been up for trying oral sex, but that wasn't on the menu. Stuart never suggested it, and as I hadn't tried it before I lacked the confidence to ask in case he rejected the idea. I had a feeling he didn't fancy 'facing up' to my miserable vulva. If I couldn't have 'real' sex, then in my eyes (and probably his) I wasn't measuring up as a girlfriend. I felt inadequate and that wasn't helping our dynamic. Stuart was patient, but I sensed his ambivalence.

My best friend was supportive, but as she'd had thrush once years ago and it had cleared up with one course of treatment I felt like a medical anomaly. I went along to the Genito-Urinary Medicine (GUM) clinic at my local hospital and had the full range of tests, but they were clear.

"Everything looks normal," said the doctor. "The pain

is all in your head. Have a glass of wine before intercourse and try and relax. Sex will get easier once you've got used to it. We'll give you some more antifungal pessaries just in case you get a flare-up of thrush."

I knew there must be more to it than that, but I was tired of trying to prove it. Instead, I bought another bottle of Glenfiddich and an eighth of hash from our local dealer in Umfreville Road and continued to grit my teeth through our occasional – and mercifully swift – attempts at shagging.

Three months after we had first met, Stuart dumped me. He told me he was still hung up about his ex-girlfriend, but I couldn't help but feel that if I had been able to perform the Karma Sutra – with an ecstatic smile on my face – he would have stuck around. I was hurt and upset and spent two months drifting in a haze of whisky and dope, writing bad poetry.

A year later, I had a short-lived relationship with Alex, a friend and ex-housemate. We attempted penetrative sex, but it still hurt like hell. I tried to explain my problem, even though I didn't really understand it myself, but Alex had insecurities of his own.

"It's because you don't really fancy me, isn't it? I don't turn you on," he lamented, limp and deflated.

It was frustrating, but eventually I got through to him. Then, unexpectedly, something transformative happened – he went down on me. Initially, I felt uncomfortable and self-conscious, but then I let go and it was bliss.

Reciprocating was just as awkward, but once I'd adjusted my technique and stopped cranking the gear-stick like Clarkson on speed, my enthusiasm paid off. Alex had a smile on his face – apparently, I had a latent talent I was unaware of. Giving head felt exciting and empowering, and I enjoyed it, which was fortunate given my 'vag' was out-of-order and it would be my sexual M.O. for years to come. Alex moved away and the relationship fizzled, but I now had a new 'menu for two' in my sexual repertoire.

There was, however, an unfortunate downside to going down. With future partners, receiving oral sex would often irritate my sensitive skin or kick-start a thrush flare-up. It's possible this was happening because enzymes that break down sugar in saliva can disrupt the vaginal microflora or alter the healthy pH of vulval tissue. This can cause skin irritation or allow thrush organisms to grow out of balance. I found that using an organic, pH-balanced lubricant afterwards was helpful in restoring the equilibrium. For most women though, with robust vulval skin and a healthy vaginal microbiome, receiving oral sex is unlikely to cause this issue[1].

Some sexually transmitted infections (STIs) can be transmitted through oral sex via skin contact or in saliva, most commonly herpes, gonorrhoea, syphilis and human papillomavirus (HPV). Less frequently, infections such as chlamydia, HIV, pubic lice and hepatitis can be passed on this way. Yet most people infected orally with an STI (other than herpes which causes visible cold sores) are unlikely to have any obvious symptoms[2].

Culturally, there has been less engagement with using protection during oral sex than during vaginal or anal intercourse, perhaps due to reduced sensitivity and pleasure, and a lack of perceived risk. The concept of using a condom is a familiar one, but dental dams are rarely spoken about beyond the sexual health clinic consulting room. These latex or polyurethane sheets can provide a barrier between the mouth and vulva or anus during oral sex but have yet to be adopted as a heterosexual norm. My newfound enthusiasm for going down had boosted my sexual confidence, but I knew I was still falling short of the real deal. The vulval pain was getting worse rather than better and weighing up the potential for pleasure versus pain was something I'd grapple with before every sexual encounter.

I went back to the GUM clinic several times, determined they would eventually find something specific they could treat, and my persistence finally paid off. I was referred to a vulval dermatologist who prescribed a mild steroid cream for my "sensitive" vulval skin. It helped a little with the soreness but did nothing for the burning pain on penetration, and I was told I couldn't have a follow-up appointment with her for nine months. I explained what I had been through over the past few years and how upsetting it had been.

"There's no need to make a fuss," she hissed. "You're not in a relationship or planning to have a baby at the moment so intercourse isn't an issue."

She looked old and withered and had a look of distaste on her face. I wondered when she had last had sex and whether she had ever enjoyed it.

Nine months later I was back again, feet in stirrups, for a review of my treatment. She strode into the examination cubicle and, without any form of greeting, snapped on some gloves and peered between my legs. I could feel hot tears welling up as I realised that to her I wasn't a person with feelings, but just another messed-up vulva on her tedious clinic round, en route to lunch.

"There's no point crying about it," she barked, "it won't help," and disappeared behind the cubicle curtain to talk to the junior doctor. It didn't occur to me to challenge her about her attitude – I was twenty-two, vulnerable, and terrified of leaving yet again without a clear diagnosis or solution.

As I listened to them discussing my case behind the curtain, I heard the term vulvodynia mentioned. During the post-exam summing-up with the junior doctor I asked what vulvodynia was – as neither of them had mentioned the term to me directly – and she explained it was a recently identified chronic pain condition. Apparently, the consultant thought vulvodynia was what I had, but there was very little they could do about it. "Try and relax and have a glass of wine before intercourse," said the junior doctor. "It may well improve on its own."

I walked, blotchy-faced, out of the hospital and into the nearest off-licence where I picked up a bottle of cheap Chardonnay and imagined how it would feel to pour it slowly over her head. I placed it back on the shelf then bought a quart of Bells, a packet of Silk Cut and a family-sized bar of Cadbury's Fruit & Nut.

Back home in my bedroom I lit up, took a swig of whisky, and scoffed half the bar of chocolate, then I threw myself on the bed and sobbed. Less than two hours ago I had been told my tears counted for nothing, but crying my eyes out felt cathartic, and afterwards an idea occurred to me; I grabbed my keys and headed for Cyberia, an internet café in Fitzrovia.

Cyberia was London's first 'cyber café' (circa 1994) and one of the few places you could connect to the internet before public and home access was rolled out. I tapped 'vulvodynia' into the search engine of a slow, grumbling PC and waited. Eventually, two mentions of the condition popped up, both in obscure American research papers. They explained what vulvodynia was and how to diagnose it, but there was no mention of a definitive cause or effective treatment.

Today, vulvodynia is defined by the UK Vulval Pain Society (VPS) as "the sensation of vulval burning and soreness in the absence of any obvious skin condition or infection" and "usually as a consequence of irritation or hypersensitivity of the nerve fibres in the vulval skin"[3]. The abnormal nerve fibre signals are felt as neuropathic pain which is often difficult to treat. Typically, neuropathic pain does not respond to over-the-counter analgesics such as paracetamol and ibuprofen. The VPS was founded in 1996 by consultant gynaecologist Dr David Nunns and nurse Diane Hamdy and continues to be the leading source of information and expertise on vulval pain in the UK.

Other factors may also be involved in triggering and perpetuating vulvodynia including overly tight pelvic floor muscles, hormonal changes (during the menstrual cycle, postpartum or menopause), mast cell activation, allergies, pudendal nerve entrapment, and genetic predisposition to chronic pain and inflammation. In some women, vaginal thrush and urinary tract infections can aggravate the sensitive vulval nerve endings and topical antifungal treatments may exacerbate the irritation. (This was certainly a causal factor for my vulvodynia, though I didn't fully understand this at the time.)

In recent years, research into the prevalence of vulvodynia indicates that it is the most common cause of pain during sexual intercourse in premenopausal women[4]. A health study carried out in the US found that as many as 16 per cent of American women may experience the condition[5]. Another study suggests it affects 8–10 per cent of women of all ages[6]. Based on current population figures, a 10 per cent prevalence equates to a massive 16.8 million women in the US and 3.5 million in the UK.

That's an enormous amount of pain and suffering, yet many women with vulval symptoms are unable to access specialist medical care, resulting in misdiagnosis and ineffective treatment.

Back in Cyberia, as I continued to read through the US research documents, my symptoms suddenly began to make sense. There appeared to be two sub-categories of the condition which, to avoid confusion, I refer to here using the latest terminology: unprovoked vulvodynia, which describes the sensation of continual vulval burning and soreness, and provoked vulvodynia – also known as vestibulodynia – which refers to pain of the vulva on light touch (particularly at the entrance to the vagina) such as with tampon use or penetrative sex. I was clearly suffering from the provoked version, but I also had regular flare-ups of soreness that lasted days or weeks at a time, which seemed to fit the unprovoked diagnosis too: a double whammy of hellfire.

But at least I now had a name for my pain, even if I didn't yet have the solution. It was a relief to know that vulvodynia was a medically-recognised condition often caused by physical nerve damage and not just some vague, unclassifiable set of symptoms – or all in my head. I was no longer a medical anomaly, a one-off freak of nature. I realised there must be other women out there with the same condition, riding the same rollercoaster of emotions, all of us searching for successful treatment.

However, connecting with them wasn't easy, as getting a vulval pain syndrome correctly diagnosed was often a tricky business. If women didn't realise they had vulvodynia – and continued to encounter ignorant doctors prescribing futile anti-thrush treatments – how could they access the medical care they desperately needed, or seek support from other women with the same condition?

My breakthrough came when I happened to see a handwritten note about a Vulval Pain Support Group on a notice board at a sexual health clinic, tucked behind NHS posters for gonorrhoea and chlamydia. I noted down the contact number and the following week after work I joined three women in a dingy hired room in Holborn. As we shared our stories, I finally felt understood after years of frustration. We swapped self-help tips and discussed the limited treatment options we had stumbled upon during our mostly futile journeys through the health system: anaesthetic gels, a TENS machine, steroid ointments, hypoallergenic wash creams and an array of alternative therapies including Chinese herbs, homeopathic pills and homemade potions.

Anaesthetic gels made my skin sting, and I would be sore for days after applying them, and other options seemed to offer minimal relief. We had very little to go on in terms of effective treatment, but sharing our frustration with each other every six weeks at least felt cathartic. The group eventually folded due to low turnout, but with the internet revolutionising communication we would later re-emerge with a bang. Hundreds of women would join our online group and we would eventually need a community hall to house our meetings as we grew in number. But for the time being, a few of us stayed in touch and we tried to manage our pain as best we could. Heartened by their support, I tried to remain optimistic about future advances in treatment, and the future advances of sexual partners.

4

A Frank encounter

After graduating, I took an administrative position at one of the University of London's colleges. It was fairly mundane, but it paid the rent while I applied for jobs in media. My friend Soraya and I would often frequent the student union bar as the drinks were cheap. The floor was sticky with spilt lager, and the smell of stale alcohol and tobacco hung in the air, a testament to perpetual nights of student excess.

One evening, we were slouched on the corner banquette, watching the university talent go by – spotty undergrads, nerdy PhDs, and the occasional demi-god blessed with magnificent physical genes to match the soaring IQ.

Suddenly, Soraya was roused from her post-work stupor.

"Jesus."

She was open-mouthed, her lips barely moving as she spoke, and she had a blank expression on her face like a ventriloquist's dummy. But somehow she was still exuding the effortless exotic beauty that made men weak at the knees.

I followed her eyes to the door. A tall and unfeasibly handsome student had just walked in. He had a mop of brown hair and was followed by his sidekick who was a couple of inches shorter but no less striking. They approached the bar with old-skool swagger, the double doors swinging behind them like hinged saloon slats in a Wild West watering hole. They might as well have been touting pistols on their hips.

The taller of the two shot a look our way and locked eyes with Soraya.

Oh God, they were coming over.

"Alright? I'm Tom."

He fired a grin at Soraya.

"And this is Marc," he added as an afterthought, without shifting his gaze from hers.

And the rest, as they say, is hindsight.

Tom was keen on Soraya from the outset. Marc was aloof at first, but after a couple of drinks he warmed up a little. He had mousey hair that flopped across his face when he raised cupped hands to light a cigarette. His faded jeans clung to him with the perfect ratio of fit to sag and screamed indie cool. Tom had on a charcoal-grey jumper which had seen better days, but it was obvious the days it had seen were quality. They both had sea-blue eyes you would happily drown in.

Tom suggested we head back to his room in the university's halls of residence, as he had a bottle of vodka and some weed. Inside his cramped bedroom, Marc and I sat crouched on the floor with our backs against the single bed, while Tom and Soraya smooched on the mattress. The desk was piled with books on anatomy – they were both studying medicine.

Marc and I chatted about music, ethics and gynaecology. Jackpot, I thought. He's beautiful, ultra cool and comfortable talking about the female reproductive system. Several drinks in, I was even up for throwing vulvodynia into the mix.

He looked puzzled. Clearly vulvodynia hadn't made it into the medical school's gynaecology syllabus.

I explained.

"So does it hurt when you have sex?" he enquired, matter of fact.

"Sometimes, not really," I lied. "Alcohol and weed numb me out." He lit another spliff, took a drag and passed it to me.

He had a rakish confidence about him, but there were hairline cracks in the glorious façade that hinted at vulnerability and damage. I was drawn to him like a moth to a flame.

Tom and Soraya indicated they wanted to be alone, so Marc and I left and walked towards the bus stop. Marc paused, as if he were about to ask me something, but suddenly his bus pulled up and he thought better of it. He mumbled a half-hearted goodbye and was gone. There was no exchange of phone numbers and I felt the sting of disappointment.

However, a week later I ran into him again at a university gig that Tom had asked Soraya along to. The two of them disappeared early on and Marc and I were left alone. Once again, he seemed detached to begin with, but as we were leaving he suddenly kissed me in the street under a flickering streetlamp. I felt myself melting; I couldn't resist and I didn't want to. I felt alive, more alive than I'd felt in a long time. We went back to his student digs – a ramshackle Victorian terrace on the other side of the river.

Although we were drunk and high, he managed to use a condom that he whipped out of a beside cabinet. I'd had some vulval symptoms over the past few days and had used an antifungal vaginal pessary the night before to ward off any possibility of thrush, just in case. Although I was sore and the sex was uncomfortable, I was anaesthetised with enough drink and dope to make it tolerable. The thrill came from the kudos of sleeping with a blue-eyed medical god, not from physical pleasure. He came, I didn't; he was indifferent.

"Er, I think the condom split," he said afterwards.

It's possible that the antifungal pessary I'd used had damaged the condom. I was unaware at the time, but topical antifungal medications can weaken latex-based condoms and diaphragms. They contain active ingredients such as polyenes, solvents, and oils which can interact with latex[1]. Oil-based lubricants (such as baby oil and petroleum jelly) have also been shown to quickly damage rubber condoms. Only water-based or silicone-based lubricants are safe to use with latex.

It's possible the condom split for another reason entirely, but either way I was bang in the middle of my menstrual cycle when ovulation occurs – the optimum time to get pregnant.

"Oh well, I've got a pharmacist mate down the road who can give you the morning-after pill tomorrow", Marc continued, blasé.

When I awoke the next morning, he was still sleeping. I wanted to feel the warmth of his skin against mine, to run my fingers down his spine and kiss his neck to wake him, but I sensed that this level of intimacy wasn't part of the unspoken deal we'd struck the night before.

When he woke up, we had sex again – without a condom. He kissed me, I melted, and suddenly he was inside me. It was the first time I'd had penetrative sex without protection. Why bother, he said, you're getting the morning-after pill.

Stone-cold sober, sex was painful, but I didn't ask him to stop. I needed him to want me, to keep on seeing me, and having real PiV (penis in vagina) sex without complaint felt like a necessary requisite for that. Instead, I tried to detach from the unwanted sensations by focusing on the contents of the room, almost out of body: a pale-skinned girl lay on a stained and crumpled duvet, while a boy with floppy hair screwed her with his eyes closed. On the bedside table, a medical textbook was propped open – an intricate drawing depicted a profusion of blood vessels, like the roots of a tree. Next to the book was a cold cup of coffee and an open tobacco tin.

Thankfully, the sex was over quickly. Afterwards, he brought me a piece of toast and marmite and then hurried me down the road to see his pharmacist friend. The emergency contraceptive I was given required two doses to be taken orally several hours apart. I swallowed one with a bottle of water then went home and took the other later.

The morning-after pill was first licensed in 1984 and had to be prescribed by a clinician, but since 2001 it has been available to buy from pharmacies, making it easier to access, though it can cost up to £30. The UK government has stated that women across England will be able to get the morning-after pill for free from pharmacies by the end of 2025. The medication contains progestogen (synthetic progesterone), or a progesterone modulator, to delay ovulation. (The hormones oestrogen and progesterone rise and fall throughout the menstrual cycle controlling ovulation and menstruation.) Levonorgestrel, which I took as a two-tablet dose, contains progestogen and has to be taken within 72 hours (three days) of having unprotected sex. Levonorgestrel's success rate varies from 57–95 per cent depending on how soon it is taken[2]. A more recent version of the morning-after pill contains ulipristal acetate, a selective progesterone receptor modulator, and can be used up to five days after contraceptive failure. Taken as a single dose, it can be up to 98 per cent effective[3].

My encounter with Marc had felt clumsy and disconnected, and I was still dealing with the burning, searing aftermath days later. On top of this, the pills made me feel horribly sick and triggered a banging headache, yet I still felt a ridiculous thrill at having slept with someone so jaw-droppingly gorgeous – one of England's elite.

Marc phoned a day later to check I'd taken the second dose. I sensed relief in his voice when I confirmed that I had. I'd felt excited when he'd asked for my number, but now I realised he just wanted to check I wasn't going to lumber him with an unwanted pregnancy. He was busy working for exams, he said, so he wouldn't be able to see me again.

My self-esteem spiralled into a nosedive, particularly as Tom was still keen to go on seeing Soraya. I was consumed by desperation. If only I could sleep with him again, I could win him over, I thought. At the very least, by sleeping with him a second time I could upgrade it from a one-night stand to a fling which, according to my warped rationale, seemed more acceptable.

Ten days later I got my chance. I had it on good authority that Marc would be at another indie gig. At first, he tried his best to ignore me, but after buying him a couple of beers I persuaded him to crash at my place which was nearby. Neither of us wanted to risk another condom breakage so instead of a shag we had a drunken 69.

A few days later, Tom told Soraya that Marc had a

girlfriend – an aspiring fashion model. She had been away travelling but was back now. Marc had cheated on her with me, and he wasn't going to risk it again. I was devastated and felt cheap and stupid. I realised now why he'd seemed ambivalent; I had been a temporary lapse of judgement.

Tom eventually lost interest too. They both went abroad on their electives, and we did our best to forget about them, but that wasn't going to be easy. Six weeks later, Soraya phoned me in tears. She had been for a routine cervical smear test, and they had delivered some unwelcome news – she had contracted genital warts.

This ubiquitous STI is caused by the human papilloma virus (HPV) which is a group of more than 200 viruses. Some cause genital warts, others are asymptomatic. Most are low risk, but some can cause cervical cancer. It is not uncommon to be infected with multiple types.

"I have to go back and be painted with this burning chemical stuff until they go away," she sobbed, "but the virus stays in your body so they might come back again, and I might be at risk of cervical cancer too. Tom and I didn't use a condom a couple of times so they must be from him."

I felt sick with fear. What if I'd picked up something from Marc? A week or so later I happened to run into Amir, one of Tom and Marc's crowd, in a local pub. I asked him if Marc slept around a lot and if I should be worried about STIs.

"Nah, course not," he said. "Marc only sleeps with classy women."

Apparently, "classy" women didn't contract STIs. I tried to feel reassured and felt an absurd sense of pride – if I'd slept with Marc I must be "classy" by association.

Still, I made an appointment at the local GU clinic to be sure. A doctor examined me. No warts, he said and the swab tests for other STIs were clear too. The relief was overwhelming. I walked home dabbing at my tears with a super-size tissue from the waiting room. I'd been given a reprieve, and I was going to make sure I didn't put myself at risk again. But my relief was short-lived.

A month on, I was back at the vulval clinic, visiting the old dragon for my now annual gynae review, to check on my vulvodynia and "sensitive skin". Her delivery was terse as always and she had some devastating news.

"See here, these are warts," she barked at the junior doctor cowering next to her. "We'll have to deal with these now as well."

I was stunned. I told her that a month ago the GU doctor had said I was fine.

"Well, I'm telling you you've got them now," she snapped.

Tears began to roll down my cheeks.

"For goodness' sake," she scoffed, "you girls will get yourselves into these situations."

She told the junior doctor to apply liquid nitrogen, a topical treatment to burn off genital warts, and to arrange for me to come back for further sessions. The liquid nitrogen was stored in a sealed black container. When the lid was removed, smoky tendrils of 'dry ice' curled upwards like a steaming witch's cauldron. The junior doctor dipped an extra-long cotton swab into the brew and got to work. It stung and burned, but it was satisfying knowing the invader was being obliterated.

I left the hospital teary and blotchy-faced and turned up the volume on my Walkman to try and drown out the turmoil in my head. I'd thought I'd got away with it, but I hadn't. On the few occasions I'd managed sex with Stuart and Alex we'd used condoms, so it had to be from Marc as I hadn't slept with anyone else. Why had I let him have sex with me without a condom? I knew I was being hard on myself – Soraya had been careless too and genital warts were a common STI. I could just as easily have contracted them from a long-term boyfriend as from Marc, but because they were a lasting reminder of my humiliating fling, I felt a searing sense of shame.

Perhaps I should tell him, I thought, be responsible. His girlfriend, and countless other women, might be infected now too. But he was abroad (mobile phones weren't yet a thing) and I was glad to have an excuse not to confront him.

At my next treatment session, I lay with my legs in stirrups once again while the junior doctor dabbed the offending areas with more liquid nitrogen from the cauldron. Afterwards, I felt in need of comfort food, and on the way home I stopped off at Cranks. This wholefood café was one of the capital's first forays into popular vegetarian grub. It sold oddities like carrot cake (we'd yet to be sold on the merits of vegetables in cake) but the chocolate sponge slathered in icing was heaven. I ordered a large slice, along with a cappuccino. I liked to think the cake's wholefood worthiness offset its calorific weight.

Through a couple of tinny ceiling speakers, Frank Sinatra was belting out big-band favourites. As I demolished my stodgy cake with a tiny recycled wooden fork, I realised I was listening to him crooning 'I've Got You Under My Skin'. Apparently, my misfortune had a soundtrack. I managed a smile, but reality soon kicked in with a vengeance.

Two months after I had finished treatment the warts returned. Thankfully, they weren't widespread or big and witchy – they were barely visible to the untrained eye – but that didn't stop me feeling ashamed and upset. Once again, I was angry with my body for letting me down. Soraya was free of them after just two treatments and they never reappeared, but apparently my immune system was failing to keep the virus under control. Over the next two years the warts continued to come and go, and a cervical smear test showed pre-cancerous cell changes. I underwent invasive procedures to remove them (including a diathermy) and two further courses of liquid nitrogen. Finally, they conceded defeat, and have never returned, and thankfully my cervical screening tests have been normal ever since.

Around 85 per cent of (unvaccinated) sexually active people will contract some form of HPV in their lifetime[5]. The body usually clears the infections eventually without recurrence, but around 50 per cent of HPV infections involve high-risk types of virus which persist and can cause cancer[6].

Cervical cancer is by far the most common HPV-related disease and around 99 per cent of cases are caused by persistent, high-risk, genital HPV infection[7]. Most cervical cancer cases diagnosed in the UK each year are in females aged 30 to 34[8]. There is also a possible causal link between oral sex, HPV, and oral and pharyngeal cancers, which are on the rise in the UK[9].

My paternal grandmother died of cervical cancer when I was four years old – more than a decade before the introduction of a nationwide cervical screening programme in 1988, which would have identified cell changes early and enabled successful treatment. Her first symptoms were abnormal vaginal bleeding. Treatment was harsh and invasive – the vaginal insertion of canisters of radium – but the cancer had spread and was terminal.

I had always viewed going for a smear test as an annoying (and potentially painful) hassle, but when my mum reminded me of how my grandmother had died I realised access to regular testing wasn't an inconvenience, it was a privilege. If pre-cancerous changes are detected early, in microscopic form, treatment is highly successful.

Since 2008, an effective HPV vaccine has been offered to all girls at the age of thirteen and in 2019 vaccination was extended to boys of the same age[10]. The nationwide UK vaccine programme is a major step towards preventing cervical cancer and possibly oral cancers from HPV exposure.

A year after I'd slept with Marc, I ran into him in a university corridor; I hadn't seen him in months.

"Hi Marc, remember me?" I proffered, with a lame attempt at a smile. I was clutching a bunch of files and a cup of tea in a hallway teeming with students, and still sickeningly weak at the knees twelve months on.

"Yeah. Hi," he responded, without conviction.

I said nothing about the warts – I was too fixated on the scab above his upper lip, which I assumed was a cold sore. A scene flashed through my head: he was going down on me in my dimly-lit bedroom while I stared at the light fitting on the ceiling. Cold sores can be passed on through oral sex to cause genital herpes. For a moment I panicked, but I didn't recall him having a cold sore during either of our sexual encounters and I hadn't had any herpes symptoms. I decided I was in the clear and heaved a sigh of relief, though it wouldn't be my last encounter with the big H. Perversely, I still fancied him – stupidly, madly, warts and all. Lust has no logic.

Twenty-five years later, I googled Marc and found his credentials on a hospital website. He is now a top consultant in his field of medicine and a highly respected lecturer at a university medical school – hopefully passing on his knowledge and expertise, rather than anything that requires medicated ointment or liquid nitrogen.

5

Liar, liar, pants on fire

My love life throughout my twenties ebbed and flowed in much the same way as my friends' relationships did, though vulvodynia had an inevitable impact. Like most of my social circle, I had the occasional fling interspersed with longer relationships that offered stability, commitment and guaranteed floral gestures on Valentine's Day. A couple of us walked up the aisle, but most of us continued to wear our hearts on our sleeves with unwavering optimism and joined the online dating revolution a decade later.

Occasional short-lived flings with exciting but non-committal men like Marc meant I could manage acute episodes of painful shagging with whisky, teeth-clenching denial and a lust-fuelled endorphin rush. Now and again, one of these liaisons would feel exciting and liberating, but mostly I was left feeling empty, sore and wracked with self-doubt, which often resulted in amped up outings of Alanis Morissette's *Jagged Little Pill*.

I also had two longer-term relationships (of 18 months and two years) with kind and considerate partners who clearly loved me enough not to make our lack of penetrative sex a deal breaker. These relationships offered a seemingly ideal setup given the limitations imposed by the vulvodynia: we stopped attempting penetrative sex, we rarely talked about the issue, and there was no real impetus to try and resolve the situation. Though flare-ups of unprovoked pain continued to fuel my search for effective treatment.

We shared "I love yous", romantic bistro dinners and holidays in the med, but beneath our apparent acceptance of the status quo there was growing tension and unease. They felt they *ought* to be able to accept the situation and I felt I *ought* to be happy to have found men who would put up with my issues, even if personality-wise we weren't a great match. But "shoulds", "ought tos" and mutual denial were a brittle foundation for real intimacy. I had perfected an 'everything but' sexual repertoire that was fun and kept our sex life alive, but I was struggling to keep the lid on the melting pot of frustration, anger and shame that was simmering inside me. I wanted the real deal – not only for my partners' benefit, or because society was telling me that penetrative vaginal sex was the heterosexual norm – but because it felt like a natural instinctive need. Sex is a primal force – the creator of life and a celebration of it. For me, PiV sex felt like a fundamental component of being human, of being a real woman. Penetration was about opening up and letting someone in deeply. This, to me, was real intimacy.

I wanted a partner with an energetic sexuality and an imagination to match my own, albeit stifled, dreams and desires. Yet my physical limitations seemed to dictate that I find a patient, sensitive man who could quell his desire for penetrative sex and that I do the same. Clearly vulvodynia didn't give me the monopoly on seeking that illusive combo of commitment, kindness and sensitivity, along with an undercurrent of wild, old-skool masculinity. This was, after all, the '90s, the decade where action-hero bravado squared up to 'New Man' sensitivity – an all-rounder who, after a smooth Gillette shave, would apply soothing post-shave balm before heading out to slay the latest threat to humanity. But my frustration ran deeper than typical twenties relationship angst. I felt muted, dimmed by my physical limitations – a ghost of the person I was capable of being. With my vagina routinely closed for business it felt as if the deep well of love, femininity and self-expression within me – that longed to flow and connect – was caught behind a roadblock.

Vulvodynia, and my relationship with it, was shaping who I was and how I interacted with the world. There were periods of relative calm when I could function day-to-day with minimum discomfort, and the burning pain was *only* present on penetration, but even during more manageable phases an exhausting inner dialogue was taking place. I was constantly checking in with how my vulva felt and the current level of discomfort – did it feel better, the same or worse than last week? What was making it feel better, worse or the same? Was it the single watered-down whisky I had allowed myself in the pub last night, or something dodgy I had eaten that was niggling it? (I had ditched the low-oxalate diet that was purported to be a cure for vulvodynia and as alcohol often triggered my bladder symptoms I'd cut my consumption to virtually nil.) Or was it the sex I had attempted last week, my choice of underwear this morning or where I was in my menstrual cycle? I was still no closer to accessing effective medical treatment and was desperately trying out more self-help measures I had heard about from the support group crew. If I thought long enough and hard enough about it maybe I would come up with a culprit, a panacea, an answer.

The soreness and burning, and my inner commentary on it, would affect my mood and ability to focus. There were very few people I was comfortable sharing the situation with so I would often appear irritable and withdrawn for no apparent reason. The anxious, frustrated voice in my head that ran on a loop in the background had begun playing into everyday decisions, emotions and experiences – in overt and obvious ways, but also with stealth and cunning. The physical pain was difficult to contend with, but my judgement of it and the way it eroded my authenticity as a woman was just as debilitating.

I was flailing wildly between overthinking, worrying and attending to my vulva's every twinge and gripe, and acute episodes of denial and distraction – wearing skin-tight jeans, buying crotch-aggravating sexy lingerie and feeding my candida with chocolate and cake – in an angry attempt to feel normal. My stress levels were at DEFCON 2 as I dealt with seemingly arbitrary flare-ups, self-imposed secrecy around the issue and my monotonous inner dialogue about it all.

Thankfully, work offered a welcome creative distraction ensuring my bank balance was healthy even if my ailing vulva wasn't. At twenty-three, I landed a job at a documentary TV channel. My colleagues were great and I loved the diverse range of programming we worked across. I was trained up to run a new magazine the company was launching, which would delve into the subjects the documentaries covered. For four years I wrote and commissioned features on everything from aerobatics and Amazonian tribes to ghosts, sharks and

Zen Buddhism. I staked-out Thetford Priory at dusk (with a cackling film crew) hoping to encounter a ghostly monk "with hot coals for eyes", looped-the-loop with a lunatic in a bi-plane, and chugged across Loch Ness at dawn (with a dreamy Welsh photographer) searching for Nessy. Eventually, with the advent of the internet, it was decided that the print publication would make way for a new website, but due to budget cuts and a marketing reshuffle, this couldn't happen for at least another year. Rather than stay on in a less interesting role, I took a redundancy deal. I thought I would have a crack at going freelance, but self-employment was far from plain sailing. Eventually, I was recommended by a colleague for a staff position on a men's style magazine – as editor of their new website. The lure of job stability and West End glamour was an enticing combo and I jumped aboard.

For six months it was a whirl of launch parties, freebies and minor celebs, but a year later the surface glitz had begun to wear thin. I was constantly at loggerheads with my boss and the ethos of the organisation and felt like a fish out of water. As I waded through the magazine's pictorials of Britain's hottest female stars, and wrote yet another banal daily blog for men riddled with sexual innuendo, I crossed my legs beneath the desk, holding on tight to my burning secret.

With Beck and Primal Scream blasting through my headphones I began coasting and doing the bare minimum, as I surreptitiously applied for other jobs. The only thing that made the situation tolerable was sharing Maltesers and office banter with my equally disillusioned co-editor. That and a flirtation with Robbie, the hot and quite possibly out-of-my-league guy on the design team.

Frustratingly, Robbie wasn't responding to my lingering looks over the photocopier; I needed to make him wake up and take notice. An impending office outing to the opening of a new nightclub seemed just the ticket, but in the run-up to the big night out my self-esteem had dipped to a new low. In the women's toilets I had encountered a gaggle of fashion-forward colleagues discussing their sexual exploits and latest designer purchases from Selfridges. Clearly my current 'image' wasn't going to cut it and I needed to seriously up my game. That's when I saw the trousers in a style magazine on reception. They were black and shiny with zips and labels and plenty of attitude.

"You'd look great in those," Phil said.

Phil was Robbie's sidekick on the design team and our gay fashion guru.

I *would* look great in those, I thought. I've just got paid; I'm going to buy them. I knew there would be consequences – the trousers were 100 per cent polyurethane and fit the model in the magazine like a second skin – but in my eagerness to impress, denial seemed a totally viable option. I had the figure for them, and what was the point if I couldn't show it off? I was going to prove that I was as good as all those girls who had paraded in front of me in skin-tight jeans over the years and the gawping models they profiled in the magazine I worked for, not to mention the willowy-blonde toilet collective. I was going to make a statement: "I'm wearing incredibly tight plastic trousers. Only a woman with a rocking figure and healthy vaginal microflora could get away with *this*."

At lunchtime I hot-footed it down to the pretentious fashion outlet listed in the magazine, and as I strutted in front of the changing-room mirror – club anthem pounding away, shop assistant looking on in admiration – I was sold. As I walked back to work, I tried to push any nagging doubts over their suitability to the back of my mind. I would deal with the consequences later. All I cared about was tonight. In this gear Robbie was going to want me badly. I wasn't going to sleep with him tonight, just have him drooling and desperate with an outside chance of low-lit snogging.

At the club they were handing out some new alcopops drink. It tasted like crap, but it was free.

"Great 'trews'," said Phil.

"Thanks," I replied. "Where's Robbie?"

"On the dance floor."

I gyrated suggestively to a top dance anthem and tried to grab Robbie's attention. He glanced my way and gave me a brief nod of recognition, and for a moment there was a flicker of hope, but it was soon dashed – I watched him leave with a blonde wearing a skirt.

After my dance floor frenzy, the trousers squelched when I walked. In the toilets I had to peel them off and blot the sweat from my legs with loo roll before I could get them up again. It was a precursor to the 'Ross's leather trousers' incident in Friends, minus the talcum powder. Clearly, I had the figure for them, but not the physiology. I had engineered the perfect conditions for a vulval meltdown.

Did I really think I could get away with my audacious fashion choice? My plan had failed in spectacular style: the skin-tight trousers were sartorial torture, and Robbie had left with another woman – one whose cooch-friendly ensemble trumped my reckless attire. The humiliation stung almost as much as my vulva did.

Still, excessive consumption of alcopops numbed the pain and the next morning I thought I'd got away with it, but by the time I'd had my mid-morning cuppa my vagina was raging: "Liar, liar, pants on fire", I could hear it screaming at me. I didn't know if it was thrush, vulvodynia or what; I just knew it hurt. The flare-up went on for a week. I swallowed an oral anti-thrush capsule, lovingly applied cooling ice packs and aloe vera gel and vowed never to wear the crotch slicers again. I was true to my word, but my vagina was sore and angry, and it wasn't going to forget this in a hurry. I was seriously screwed, but sadly not by Robbie.

The meltdown in my trousers was followed a couple of months later by a full-on health meltdown, as I continued to push myself to feel good enough in an environment I felt suffocated by. One hectic week in May, I was frantically trying to meet a deadline for the magazine at the same time as producing a last-minute presentation for the final interview stage of another job (a position I didn't really want as it was a role in commercial rather than creative media, but I was desperate to move on and it paid double my current salary). Whilst juggling the pressure of both deadlines I was also doing battle with my boss over something mind-numbingly trivial and fighting off a fluey bug (I'd come down with numerous viral infections over the past year).

At 9 a.m. that Tuesday morning my head was pounding and I ached all over, but I was optimistic my habitual cocktail of caffeine, Nurofen Plus and dogged resilience would see me through. By 11 a.m., though, things weren't going to plan – I felt dizzy and fatigued, the office noise and screen-glare felt overwhelming, and I hurt all over. I was sent home and told to get some rest.

I remember leaving the office with a packet of Maltesers and the flapjack I had picked up from a café on St Christopher's Place on the way in. I was wearing a yellow dress from Jigsaw and black boots from Office. Strange the trivial details we remember about pivotal days in our lives; days which seem inconsequential at the time, yet become indelibly imprinted on the psyche. I remember the security guy on the front desk saying there's a bug doing the rounds, you'll be over it by the weekend. I had no idea I was leaving the building for the last time, or that it would be seven years before I would be well enough to walk into town to buy a magazine, let alone work for one again.

6

Scrounging and lounging

The weekend came and went. This bug that was doing the rounds was a total bastard. Just walking to the bathroom or the fridge felt like wading through treacle; I ached all over and even rolling over in bed required monumental effort. My mind was sluggish and foggy, and thoughts had become indistinct shapes looming in the smog.

Days passed with no change. I was looking forward to a friend's party at the weekend, and although work was a drag I missed the banter. I was done with bed rest and lying semi-comatose in front of *The Jerry Springer Show*. A healthy dose of normality and sheer force of will would kick this bug's sorry viral arse. I hauled myself out of bed and headed to the corner shop for a newspaper. Tomorrow I would go back to work and on Saturday night any remaining viral stragglers would drown in a torrent of whisky and soda.

I just about made it to the newsagent's but my leg muscles hurt like hell, and by the time I got home I felt as though I'd run a marathon. I was totally wiped out and had to sit and rest on the stairs before I could make it up to the flat. I slumped on the sofa but I couldn't focus properly on the newspaper. The chatter on the TV, and even the sunlight streaming through the window, felt overwhelming. This didn't feel like typical post-bug malaise; it was total sensory overload. Exhausted, I crashed out in bed for three hours, but couldn't sleep. My mind was buzzing and whirring like an over-exerted PC stuck in screen freeze, unable to function yet also unable to shut down.

That night, like many nights to follow, my sleep was fitful and punctuated by strange and exhausting dreams, which on waking I couldn't fully recall or make sense of; that perplexing post-dream state of almost grasping something just out of reach like a word on the tip of the tongue. A couple of dreams I did remember took the form of twisted Tim Burton-esque fables, strewn with references to childhood fairytales – glass slippers, a red cloak and sleeping for a hundred years. I had the unsettling sense of something rising up through me that was beyond my conscious comprehension.

The next morning, I awoke feeling slightly better, but by lunchtime the tidal wave of fatigue had crashed in again. My whole being felt contaminated, as if poison were pulsing through my veins. My muscles were sore, my head and neck hurt, and I had an aching heaviness in my legs which worsened whenever I attempted to move from sofa to fridge to bathroom.

And so it went on, for weeks – feeling perpetually crap despite rest and recuperation, fresh air, multivitamins and determined attempts to just get the hell over it. I tried again to walk to the shop; a friend drove me to a café for a cuppa and a pep talk; I had work sent home in an attempt to get back in the swing. But even if I managed brief exposure to 'normal', I'd pay later and plummet into a worse state than before I'd had the audacity to bother. The symptoms refused to respond to force, surrender or coercion.

I began another frustrating journey through the medical system. The GP did blood tests, but nothing showed up. I was referred to a neurologist for more tests, but long before I got the official diagnosis, I had already sussed what was wrong. It felt familiar, this aching, grinding exhaustion, yet far worse this time around. Back in '85 it had been dubbed 'Yuppie Flu' after the 'Yuppies' it often affected (Young Upwardly Mobile Professionals) – a scourge of the ambitious. Then it became Myalgic Encephalomyelitis (ME), also known as Chronic Fatigue Syndrome (CFS), which also has symptoms in common with fibromyalgia. More recently, another shiny new title was proffered – SEID, or Systemic Exertion Intolerance Disease. But whatever you want to call it (and KNACKERED might well be the best descriptor) it's a sly and devastating illness.

A frustrating secondary symptom was also about to kick in – other people's judgement. Although my family and the majority of my friends were supportive, though frustrated, at my inability to bounce back, there were a few choice acquaintances who disappeared off the radar once they had dropped hints about malingering and attention seeking. And then there was the wider public perception. ME was, and still is, viewed by many as a beige, market-stall knock-off of an illness. A condition fabricated by a neurotic, entitled, underclass intent on a life of scrounging and lounging – all ambition and motivation flushed down the pan. It's a view that has been touted for decades by sceptical media pundits who are adamant we should just get some fresh air and exercise and get over ourselves. A well-known newspaper columnist once declared that if a bunch of people with ME had to survive on a desert island she bet they would snap out of it, find the energy and get on with staying alive.

Then there's the comedy value. A popular stand-up comic observed with a snigger that apparently no-one in Africa has ME – no-one ever says they can't go to the well for water because they're knackered. I doubt Africa's malnourished ever say "I can't go to the well, I'm depressed" either, but as depression and bipolar are now more widely recognised and endorsed by a gaggle of cool celebs, mental health is less of a soft target. From Stephen Fry and Ruby Wax to Cara Delevingne and Billie Eilish, depression and neurodiversity are all the rage, and hats off to them for raising awareness of mental health issues through discussion of their personal experiences. ME on the other hand has the kind of celebrity quotient that would struggle to get booked for a double-glazing ad, let alone lead a PR rebrand. Where are the cool and kooky celebs to haul ME from the murky well of controversy[1]? At home knackered, presumably.

If I hadn't experienced the illness myself, perhaps I would be sceptical too. From the outside, ME can seem wishy-washy and vague. There may be no obvious trigger for onset, and there is still no medical test to confirm its presence; ME is a diagnosis of exclusion and there is no medically proven treatment that works for everyone. The World Health Organization states that there is "no consensus agreement amongst medical professionals as to how CFS may be definitively diagnosed"[2].

Action for ME, a UK support organisation, defines the illness as long-term and fluctuating with symptoms affecting many bodily systems: "People with ME experience debilitating pain, fatigue and a range of other symptoms associated with post-exertional malaise, the body and brain's inability to recover after expending even small amounts of energy"[3]. It affects an estimated 250,000 people in the UK, and around 17 million people worldwide[4].

In 2021, The National Institute for Health and Care Excellence (NICE) published clearly defined diagnostic criteria and recommendations for treating the illness[5], but medical opinion is still divided as to its cause and categorisation: Is it triggered by a virus? Is it a neurological or an immune system condition? Is it physiological or psychological? Then there's the vast spectrum of difference in severity, experiences and outcomes. ME has become an umbrella term for a broad and diverse group of patients from the terminally bedbound to high-functioning boom and busters. Symptoms can also vary hour-to-hour, day-to-day. People can't understand how they saw you in a café yesterday (God forbid, smiling like a well person) yet today you're bedbound and barely functioning. They get really tired sometimes too they say.

Perhaps it's easier to look at what ME is not and put some myths to sleep. I wasn't clinically depressed and this wasn't lethargy, apathy or an excuse not to go to work. Okay, I wasn't happy at work, but not to the degree that I would consciously drop out for a life of housebound tedium and austerity. I loved my holidays, my Soho dinners and my shopping excursions too much, and I had been in the final stages of securing another job.

As the illness progressed, I started having weekly sessions with a psychotherapist as a means of support. We would often speak over the phone as travelling to see her would wipe me out. It was a relief to be able to vent my frustration to someone outside of family and friends and I gained some useful insights into core issues and patterns of behaviour, but therapy did zero for the ME symptoms.

I wasn't experiencing panic attacks or agoraphobia, nor was this some neurotic state of crapness I was indulging in that I lacked the moral stature to overcome. ME is not a character flaw or a moral failing, though boy did it start to feel like one as I became my harshest critic – "snap out of it", "pull yourself together". Push, push, push.

Imagine another year in and out of work, I thought, like that failed O-level year in '85. I couldn't do that again, I refused to do that again, but time didn't give two figs and marched on regardless. Weeks became months, cracks began to form, and soon there were huge, gaping holes where 'I' used to be. After three months off sick, I was sacked from work. I siphoned what savings I had into rent, bills and private medical care in a bid to beat lengthy NHS waiting lists. The standard medical treatment for ME was a programme of graded exercise, cognitive behavioural therapy and nutritional support. I was also offered a low-dose tricyclic antidepressant to help my broken sleep (trimipramine, as amitriptyline – the first-line treatment – had debilitating side effects). Tricyclics must be taken in much higher doses to treat depression, but small amounts can be useful in calming the nervous system and helping with sleep. I certainly slept better, but the other symptoms remained.

Then reality began to bite; the money ran out – I would have to enter the welfare system. I filled out the forms for Incapacity, Housing, and Council Tax benefits, and Disability Living Allowance. An assault course in bureaucracy, which would involve a lengthy and exhausting trek through the appeals and a tribunal process, as I tried to navigate through a system that viewed disability as black and white, with little capacity for beige.

Along with my finances, my social life and self-esteem were also dwindling. I needed something, or someone, to grab hold of to stay afloat. Enter Gareth, the friend of a former work colleague, and my self-appointed human life raft. As he had also had ME, and was now recovering well, it was suggested that I might like to call him for advice and support.

Gareth was a woodturner and lived out in the sticks in a stone cottage. This gave him an air of earthy romance à la D.H. Lawrence. Woodturner, I decided, fell into the same category as blacksmith, stonemason and game-keeper. He made bowls and candleholders and crafty stuff from chunks of beech and ash and – I would later discover – smelt of wood shavings and wax polish, which added a sensual top note to the mix.

We gabbed on the phone and hit it off immediately. I needed to be rescued and he needed a renewed sense of purpose in life – it was a match made in plywood. He came to London to see me and a couple of weeks later I got overexcited and attempted the train journey out to the country. I lay slumped across the seats, utterly knackered. By the time I arrived I was barely functioning; even holding a conversation was a struggle and I had to crash out under the duvet for 24 hours. It would soon become apparent that 'going out' with someone when you can't actually go out would prove to be something of a challenge. Staying in wasn't a whole lot of fun either, particularly as the vulval pain was flaring up big time and penetrative sex was a no-go. (Gareth hid it well, but would later reveal that on top of dealing with my ME status, he was "freaked out by the whole vulvodynia thing".)

Still, we gave it a go, hanging out, chatting and cooking gluten-free feasts of health mush. All the while his matted, obese cat looked on with disdain, plotting my demise. We managed a few more get-togethers from summer into autumn and he spent Christmas with me at my parents' place, but the end was nigh. On my second and final trip down over New Year, we watched DVDs and listened glumly to his collection of New Age chill, as he stroked the sly, distended cat. His simpering feline was getting way more attention than my ailing pussy.

A cold front had begun to move in and I sensed the darkness of an impending internal winter. Gareth began to back away into his woodshed 'cave' with his fawning sidekick. I reminded him, he said, of when he was ill and he couldn't go back there; reliving it through me was too painful.

And so the inevitable happened; he finished with me – on New Year's Eve, as I lay semi-comatose on his sofa, half an hour before the fireworks went off on the BBC. On New Year's Day my parents rolled up and bundled me into the car. As they drove me back to the family home, I lay on the back seat and sobbed.

7

Stockholm syndrome

Gareth had been my raincoat and my silver lining. Now he was gone, all that remained was a dark cloud and a sense of foreboding. Six months into my illness and with no end in sight, I was struggling to cope.

I was still having weekly sessions with my psychotherapist, but talking things over was just amplifying the pain. I was crumbling, and the mess that was left felt unsafe and unlovable. Sally Turner had left the building. Her warmth and wit, and her creativity and resourcefulness were alien to me. It felt as though my tough outer skin – the Whistles wardrobe, the quips and the media savvy – had been stripped back like one of von Hagens' bodies in the Tate; my nerves and inner wiring exposed and vulnerable to the ravages of the world.

The bouts of crying were becoming more and more frequent and if I was left in a room on my own the sobbing would start from nowhere and wouldn't stop. Alone, I felt undefined and adrift. I needed another human being to provide context, to remember that I was a person and not just boundless emotion.

The reassuring touch of my brother's hand or the nuzzle of Alfie, our scruffy family dog, would bring me back into my body, which was a momentary comfort. But then I would realise with a jolt that I was trapped once again inside what was left of 'Sally Turner 1.0 '. I wanted out, or at the very least I wanted an upgrade to a better version; I needed my brain defragged and new software installed, a state-of-the-art immune system, and a brand new 'designer vagina'. Stuck inside this plodding, defunct operating system I could feel panic and claustrophobia setting in. I wanted to scream, but instead the howl turned inwards.

Depression has long been referred to as 'the black dog', which seems an incongruous metaphor given we are a nation soft on pooches. A black dog is a snoozing labrador lolling at my feet in front of an open fire, twitching with dreams of rabbits, soft ears awaiting a ruffle. The darkness that had begun to stalk me was the antithesis of this comforting and benign scenario. It felt malevolent, like the sinister unseen entity in a horror movie, or the 'black cancer' of cult '90s *X-Files*; always there, lurking in my periphery vision, feeding on what little strength I had left, waiting to emerge and engulf me.

The entity had an agenda. It wanted to bring me to my knees, slowly and painfully, in a bespoke torture chamber of my own making. Chameleonic, it shape-shifted between melancholy, anxiety, catastrophising and vitriolic self-hatred. Each day, water-boarded by my own tears, I would almost drown, but not quite; engulfed by violent emotions then caught in agonising mental paralysis, unable to function or make the simplest of decisions. My imagination, once my inspiration and guiding light, was turning on me, warping my fears and weaknesses and playing them out in a grim showreel, my eyes pinned open like *A Clockwork Orange*.

Every morning I would awake with a jolt to the maddening drip-drip of self-reproach, my airline sleep mask a makeshift blindfold. Then the interrogation would begin: How could I have let this happen? Why wouldn't my body and mind respond to my will? Why couldn't I beat the dark thoughts and leaden exhaustion, and sort out my messed-up vagina while I was at it? The answer was always the same – because I wasn't good enough, because I lacked the grit and the backbone and the A1 genes to thrive in this Darwinian survival of the fittest. Then the projector would flicker into motion, splicing together gruesome random images from a mental stash of sick fantasies, hearsay, and horror trailers: how would I feel if Alfie got run over – his legs bent and broken, his skull crushed by a car that had failed to stop? What would be the easiest way to die, or the most gruesome way to go? How would it feel to drown, or to slit my wrists in Gareth's bathtub, the blood oozing and clouding the warm water as I slipped into welcome oblivion? Who would come to my funeral and who would just send trite condolences?

I could still separate from these thoughts, but continuing to live this way felt unbearable. Then the dark presence would shape-shift once more, changing tack, whispering softly to me through the pain like a siren – calling me towards my demise. Stockholm syndrome was setting in; I had begun to fall for my tormentor and I was drifting out to sea in a rowing boat, cloaked in velvet darkness. With each passing day the shore was getting further and further away. The voices of friends and family and the drone of the TV became ever more distant as I slipped towards the horizon, the edge of the world. It felt perversely enticing this voyage towards the abyss. Part of me wanted to be sucked out and under, to let go; seduced by the magnetic pull of my negative polarity.

As I glanced back, I could still make out the faint glimmer of hope. A beacon was shining through the mist, lit up like Brighton pier, emblazoned with a slogan: *PROZAC by Eli Lilly*. I didn't want to take an antidepressant. Okay, I was already taking a tiny amount of a tricyclic drug to help me sleep, but taking the full whack to treat depression was confirmation that I couldn't just pull myself together like the Darwinian elite. But I knew that without medication I would bring the people I loved down with me; my world would end not with a bang but with a whimper, and a bitter protracted moan. Long before things escalated to suicide and blood in the bathtub, I would most likely bore myself to death with self-loathing, daytime soaps and Countdown, slipping into a state of terminal greyness and mediocrity that would taint everyone around me.

My family were already showing signs of contamination. They looked worn and weary, reflecting back my anxiety and pain like a hall of mirrors. I couldn't bear to see them hurting, knowing that I was the cause, but I was in no state to return to the flat in London. With unstinting patience they tried in vain to fix me. Mum frantically tried to bake me better with pies, cakes and puddings, and drove me to see private doctors and specialists, all paid for from my parents' dwindling savings. My brother would drive over after work and, at my request, take me on excursions to dark blustering car parks on Surrey Heath, where the rain would beat on the windows and I could rant and sob in the padded safety of his Nissan Micra. He would listen without judgement, holding my hand, telling me he loved me no matter what. He understood how it felt, this spiralling downwards; we shared the same nature and nurture, the same brain chemistry, and for the rest of our lives we would be guardians and barometers of each other's head space.

Whilst I was in the throes of depression, my father's health was also deteriorating. Soon after he retired from teaching at sixty-five, he had been diagnosed with Parkinson's disease. It was a shock to us all; I couldn't remember him having so much as a cold when I was growing up – physically he had always looked healthy, lithe and athletic, despite smoking thirty Silk Cut a day. We had first noticed something was wrong when the The *Daily Telegraph* began to shake and rattle in his hands as he read. Then his six-foot-two frame began to crumple and he took on the characteristic shuffling gait and the blank, haunted stare indicative of Parkinson's. At seventy-three, he could no longer drive, cut up his own food, dress or wash himself; Mum was his dexterity and his lifeline.

One evening as I ran a bath, tears streaming down my face, he appeared around the half open door. We sat on the edge of the bath together, and he took my hand. I knew he was crying too, though we didn't look at each other, knowing that if we did the emotional dam we had spent years constructing might break.

He was shaking and his voice cracked as he spoke:

"I love you very much and I would do anything to make this better for you."

We both knew there was nothing he could do. He could no longer fix my problems with a bag of coconut ice or the promise of a happy ending, but the fact that he wanted to was enough.

"I love you too."

The words felt awkward. We weren't used to letting the depth of what we felt for each other surface.

Growing up, I had begun to feel smothered by the closeness we had shared when I was a child. His caring had begun to feel anxious and cloying and to weigh heavily on my plans, keeping me in girlhood when I wanted to be a woman; the crown he had worn as king of my world lay crumpled on the floor. As I entered my teens, I was angry with him because, instinctively, I felt he was faking it. He had fed me a lie for years and I had believed it; the lie of happily ever after. That everything works out in the end and there is always a silver lining; that love endures and there is always something better around the corner. It was his sticking plaster for every problem, large or small, but I had x-ray specs and beneath the warmth and the wit and the unswerving optimism I sensed a darkness and sadness in him that he would never speak of. Why should I feel buoyed up by his pseudo optimism when he was struggling to believe it himself? Yet perched with him there, on the side of the bath, there was no parental PR spin or sugar-coating. It felt real.

My family were a huge support, but the time had come to bite the bullet. I popped the first pill from the blister pack and waited to get happy. My neurologist had prescribed 20 mg of Seroxat (paroxetine), an SSRI antidepressant which he said was better for "ME brains" than Prozac, whatever that meant. He had told me it might take a fortnight or so to kick in, but after a week the crying stopped suddenly, as if an off-switch had been flicked. I could focus and felt buffered against the world again, as if I had an invisible deflection shield like the Starship Enterprise in *Star Trek*. Less welcome was the odd glitching and flashing sensation I was experiencing, rather like a TV signal breaking up, and I felt wired and buzzy in the evenings which meant upping the tricyclic to help me sleep.

What the drug failed to do was help my chronic fatigue symptoms or vulval pain, though there were those who were determined it should. Perhaps I had been depressed all along and ME and vulvodynia were just physical representations of that? Now my brain chemistry was sorted, surely I'd be able to get my body back in sync too, mind over matter. A couple of years later, friends got overexcited about Charlotte's "depressed vagina" in *Sex and the City*, and desperately wanted mine to perk up too. Vulvodynia had been outed on HBO and Charlotte's vulval pain was magicked away by a course of antidepressants, then it was back to business as usual, banging Kyle McClachlan from *Twin Peaks*.

SSRIs such as Prozac (fluoxetine) and Seroxat (paroxetine) are not a first-line treatment for vulvodynia; it is tricyclic antidepressants that are sometimes useful in managing neuropathic pain. I continued to take a low-dose tricyclic at night as its sedative effect helped my disturbed sleep, but I couldn't tolerate the higher levels being touted for the treatment of vulvodynia. Upping the level turned me into a constipated zombie; I could barely string a sentence together or move from my bed.

Although the antidepressants were not a magic bullet for all my ills, the 'happy pills' were working to a degree and the depression had slipped back into the shadows. SSRIs had put me in the mid zone – able to cope again, and to focus enough to read, to hold a meaningful conversation, to search for new treatments and to reconnect with my libido. But in doing so they had cut off both ends of the spectrum – the agony and the ecstasy. For several weeks I couldn't cry; my brain would react to an emotional trigger, but the tears wouldn't flow. Eventually, my tears began to trickle again, but the drug had stemmed the flow. At the other end of the spectrum, I couldn't reach orgasm either. My sex drive had been deadened by the depression, but had begun to re-emerge. I was reading Nancy Friday's erotic fiction under the duvet and enjoying fantasies of my own, but try as I might, I couldn't hit the jackpot. Reaching orgasm had always been swift and easy; I had been able to override sexual pain with pleasure and a mind-blowing endorphin rush. Losing this pinnacle of sexual expression was devastating. Eventually, weeks later, I managed to get there, but it would take forever. I would be rubbing away feverishly, waiting for the genie to pop, at risk of repetitive strain injury and missing the beginning of *Family Affairs*.

Still, these unwanted side effects were a price I was willing to pay for mental stability. Now that depression had taken a back seat, the drive to find successful treatments for the ME and the vulval pain had returned. I had tried conventional approaches without success. Now I was willing to search for answers off the beaten track, and I was about to take a very bizarre turn down Woo-Woo Street.

8
Woo-Woo Street

Everyone has a line when it comes to complementary medicine – a dividing line that also dissects the controversial realms of the paranormal, the spiritual and the unexplained. On one side there is what we believe to be true, or are at least open to considering. On the other, well, that's just plain crazy. Why would anyone believe that shit?

Nothing divides a room like woo-woo. In the immortal words of spirit medium Derek Acora, from TV's *Most Haunted*, "For those who believe, no proof is necessary. For those who do not, no proof is possible"[1]. For Mulder, custodian of *The X-Files*, "the truth is out there"[2], but mostly it's in here, inside our heads, loaded with judgement and smug subjective bias.

I had a line, and I was about to cross it. Frustrated by western medicine's inability to heal me, I began to look to complementary therapies for answers – a quest that would run in parallel with spiritual seeking. This was a road well-travelled, the oft trodden path of the chronically ill, the desperate and the frustrated, hope forever glowing orb-like on the horizon. If I was going to come to terms with my life now and its unexpected downturn, I needed a broader perspective. I needed to find a deeper meaning in what was happening and to turn this experience into something creative, transformative and useful. Life is unfair, shit happens, and then you die, wasn't going to cut it.

I began to ask the age-old questions: Why am I here? Why am I suffering? Am I more than the sum of my broken body and mind? My dwindling health and finances wouldn't support *Eat, Pray, Love* air miles, but thanks to a listening library of audio books, cut-price therapists-in-training, and the good will of many, I was on the road. My health issues might prevent me from jetting off and exploring the world at large, but I was about to begin a journey inward as extraordinary as any trip I might make on Qantas, and with no limit for excess baggage.

Long before branded New Age spirituality appeared on my radar, religion and the spiritual had weaved their way through my formative years. Growing up, I had a strong sense of a life force – the animating energy that flows through creativity, emotions and the natural world. This innate wisdom felt separate to the God of school assemblies, who often seemed detached and irritable, an authority figure fixated on rules and regulations. As a child it was clear that being a 'good girl' proffered rewards and approval. But once the hormonal rush of puberty had kicked in, being bad could feel exceedingly good, and any twinges of guilt often added to the frisson. I had a hazy karmic notion that what goes around comes around, though it also seemed to me that good people weren't always happy or rewarded for their virtues, and that people behaving badly often got away with it and moved up in the world. Life was unfair and more than a little confusing.

We weren't regular church goers, but Christianity and The Lord's Prayer had a powerful impact on my childhood psyche. Five days a week, I would listen to my father recite The Lord's Prayer during our school assemblies – up on stage from behind a sturdy wooden lectern. Afterwards, he would hand out sweets from a huge tub of Quality Street to children who were celebrating birthdays. He loved the purple ones, and it was an ongoing joke that the children must never choose those. If a child was ever brave enough to pick one, Dad would gasp in mock horror and the audience would roll about laughing. At five years old, the language of The Lord's Prayer made little sense to me; apparently God made "art in heaven" and I had no idea what "hallowed be thy name" meant, or what "trespasses" were, but it sounded serious. Its strangeness was offset by the warmth of my father's voice, and in memory it is synonymous with bright purples, golds and greens, the colours of shiny sweet wrappers.

As a child I believed vicars were wizards, casting spells on newlyweds at the altar to bless them with children. How else could you explain how children were created? I had noted variations in the size of families, so clearly some spells (and certain vicars) were more potent than others. Later I took my cues from Mum who had a bespoke faith, but little time for 'holier than thou' types who swanned about in a snooty, churchy clique. If going to heaven meant spending all eternity with that lot, she would joke, then she would rather be "chased around hell with a toasting fork". As I entered my teens, we shared an interest in the mysterious and the unexplained, which overlapped as much with the edge of science and mysteries of the mind as it did with the spiritual. And I found people's secrets, quirks and eccentricities as fascinating as anything strange out there in the woods, the oceans or the ether.

Now, at thirty, I was crossing the arbitrary line I had drawn between truth and nonsense and was open to trying pretty much anything that might, somehow, make me well. I tried therapies aimed at treating specific health issues and also made valiant attempts to realign my entire system in one go – mind, body and spirit. Perhaps I could deal with ME, vulvodynia, depression and an ingrowing toenail in one holistic hit. I went for acupuncture, homeopathy, reiki and reflexology; I sat in sitz baths of pungent Chinese herbs, inserted crystal dildos, and lay back and thought of England during a grim and windswept colonic cleanse. From spiritual healing to holographic re-patterning, from journey therapy to space clearing, I tried it all with unflinching optimism.

When my health would support it, I rocked up at gatherings of the well-meaning well and the ever-hopeful sick – a motley crew of empaths, eccentrics and the quietly ordinary, who would gather in incense-filled living rooms behind voile curtains and a veneer of selfless serenity. I'd get a lift to a healing circle or a crystal recharge session, where participants would speak in languid whispers and cradle big chunks of quartz, caressing them like lapdogs. On one occasion, I clasped a mug of detox tea and prayed for sweet release, as the woman next to me waxed on about what a bind it was to be gifted with psychic insight. Apparently whilst shopping in Waitrose she would suddenly sense a dense aura around another customer and have to send them unconditional love and light in the condiments aisle.

Barmy as these gatherings often were, they offered a sense of connection with the mystical, so long as I curbed my cynicism and bypassed the egos and semantics. Here, each personal journey had meaning; life was about learning, healing and transformation, unfettered by the constraints of body, mind and mortality. Complementary medicine did what it said on the tin; it complemented standard medical options, providing a holistic approach to illness that also recognised the emotional, psychological and spiritual aspects of wellbeing, alongside the purely physical. The complementary practitioners I met were great listeners and empaths, and the time, energy and compassion they showed me as a client was a welcome contrast to some of the prickly medically-trained doctors I had encountered over the years. I felt held by their care and optimism, and I began to feel that I had the potential to expand and grow despite my physical limitations.

During my spiritual salvage hunt, one set of experiences stood out from the rest and inspired an ongoing fascination with the interrelationship between mind and body. One morning, I watched a woman on a daytime TV show being regressed under hypnosis to a 'past life' by a therapist who I'll call Freya – an experience that appeared to shed light on her current health issues and which generated specific personal and historical information that apparently had a basis in fact when researched. It seemed incredible, but I was intrigued and visited her website to book a session.

On a drizzly afternoon, I got a cab to Freya's flat in Putney – a calm, rose-infused haven. She had an air of spiritual authority, softened by a tumbling mane of auburn hair, and spoke in breathy, whispered tones that had me transfixed. I wanted to open up my subconscious and have her massage it gently, which I imagined would be akin to having my scalp tickled by one of those deconstructed hand whisk thingies they sell in alternative-gift stores. Once we began the process, though, I felt pangs of concern. This would be the first time I had gone under hypnosis. What if I connected with something traumatic – real or imagined – that my conscious mind couldn't cope with? Or what if I was so pathologically wired that I couldn't relax into a hypnotic state and nothing happened at all?

In the hope that whatever came up would shed some light on my vulvodynia, Freya decided to focus the regression via the base and sacral chakras (which are said to influence our sexual energy and wellbeing.) For twenty minutes, as I closed my eyes and drifted, Freya attempted to lead me into an altered state. Nothing happened.

But then, suddenly, in a fleeting moment of stillness amid the mind chatter, I felt the odd sensation of dropping. Flashes of colour, images and events began to unfold before me, along with intense feelings and emotions. This didn't feel dreamlike. I felt fully awake yet had a strange dual sense of awareness; I could still hear Freya's voice asking me questions, yet I had slipped into another world and I was looking through another set of eyes. I had assumed that if this worked I would 'remember' a lifetime in which I was a woman who had experienced something sexually traumatic; something that might explain my current symptoms of vulval pain. Instead, I 'woke up' as a man, in Cardiff, in 1837, to a tale of the unexpected:

"In front of me is what looks like a furnace – I can feel the intense orange heat as I place something inside it using a long metal pole. My name is John and I'm thirty-four years old. Am I a blacksmith? Or perhaps it's an oven and I'm a baker? How I make my living feels unimportant in this moment, as my attention is on the doorway. Standing there is a young

man in a blue uniform with gold buttons. He's a soldier and his name is Nicholas. He has deep blue eyes and brown hair that curls a little at the nape of his neck. His presence is deeply affecting and I feel a thrill and an attraction that surpasses anything I have ever felt before.

Now we're in the back storeroom. Nicholas is bent over a workbench. I'm behind him, inside him. It's the first time I've had sex with a man and the joy I feel, the sense of release, is overwhelming. Beyond erotic desire, I feel a deep sense of emotional fulfilment. I didn't know this joy, this intensity of feeling, was possible. I want to shout it from the rooftops: 'I am free, I am truly alive'. I sense the strength and power of my body against his, the ecstasy of our combined masculinity. I am a man connecting with another male, and it feels profoundly moving.

I have slept with women but always felt a sense of emptiness and disconnection; I enjoyed their company but something was missing. I have always known that I would never marry.

Now we're on horseback, galloping through woods and open countryside, whooping with the thrill of speed and the pure joy of being alive together.

Twenty years have passed. I am sitting alone in a tavern. I haven't seen Nicholas for years but there is no bitterness, only a deep sense of gratitude for the time we had together. I am about to keel over from a heart attack, but I am content to go – I have lived a full and happy life and loved deeply."

Freya's voice brought me back into the present. As I opened my eyes I had a sense that something profound had shifted emotionally. I felt a sense of relief, as if an emotional weight had been lifted. But how could accessing my supposed experiences as a gay man in 1837 help heal my vulval pain in 2003?! Freya suggested that I had perhaps tapped into that lifetime as a healing mechanism, because as John my sexual energy could be expressed freely without pain. It was best, though, to let my subconscious integrate the experience, she added, rather than dwelling on it and consciously trying to make sense of what had occurred.

But letting go wasn't easy. When I left Freya's place, I was still alive with the erotic charge I had felt as John. Back home, I pulled back the covers, jumped into bed and began reliving my tryst with Nicholas. In my mind's eye I was John, but this time I was experiencing the sexual encounter through a female body. This sense of ecstatic connection lasted for several days then slowly ebbed away.

I felt instinctively that what I'd experienced during the regression was real – that I had lived it. But it wasn't long before overthinking and cynicism kicked in. The experience was littered with Freudian metaphor. Surely this was just a case of 'penis envy' and suppressed, frustrated desire? I was a woman with a history of sexual health problems. Had my subconscious tried to liberate me from years of vulval pain by conjuring up a vagina-free zone, a dreamlike safe haven where I could experience sexual fulfilment in a different context? And then there was the imagery – reaching into the heat, perhaps to put 'a bun in the oven'. An unconscious desire for pregnancy? Or perhaps had I tapped into Jung's collective unconscious and latched on to an instinct or archetype I needed to connect with, in order to heal emotionally in some way – rather than remembering an actual past life. The cultural psychology module of my media degree came flooding back and now had a practical application I hadn't anticipated.

On another occasion, a further regression with Freya

appeared to make sense of my ME symptoms. Again I was male, this time in the Dordogne region of France, in 1498. Following the experience, I remained emotionally connected, this time with an overwhelming sense of despair and exhaustion, which stayed with me for several days. When I got home I googled the region's coat of arms which I had seen under hypnosis. There it was, on the screen in front of me – three yellow lions on a red heraldic shield.

My 19th-century Welsh fling became an anecdote I'd reel out years later at dinner parties – the gay baker from Cardiff. Yet, at the time, it had been profoundly moving. Making light of it was my way of processing something that was clearly considered wacko by the hard science contingent sitting opposite. Of course I could've picked up references from both regressions unconsciously from books, TV or an overheard conversation; I knew that was the most rational explanation, but even if these experiences were 'waking dreams' rather than past lives, I was awestruck by what the mind is capable of, and by what the subconscious constructs in an attempt to liberate us from illness, pain and upset.

These regression experiences were more deeply felt than anything I had experienced through psychotherapy or any aspect of healing, complementary or mainstream. I was intrigued by the relationship between our subconscious mind and our physiology; how mind and body intertwine and communicate whilst we are nonchalantly unaware. We remain wedded to the incessant drone of the conscious mind, as an intense and clandestine liaison is taking place behind the scenes. I felt this subconscious energy, which flowed through my dreams, my pain and 'past lives', was trying to tell me something – or perhaps

I was imposing meaning upon it – either way, I felt a positive sense of momentum. This was the flow of the intangible; the life force that had always felt impossible to tame or to fully articulate.

However, although the regression had felt emotionally powerful, this and the numerous other complementary therapies I tried had no perceptible healing effect on the vulvodynia, ME or depression. My health issues stubbornly refused to shift, though the antidepressant was doing a good job of keeping me afloat. A few years later, I would find an alternative therapy that would have a remarkable impact on my ME symptoms, but for now the 'magic bullet' remained elusive.

During my time on the road I'd had numerous tour guides and had dipped into guidebooks that were inspiring and trite in equal number, but the words that resonated were those of Sufi mystic Rumi: "the wound is the place where the light enters you"[3]. I had my sore spots, physical and emotional, but where pain had cracked me open, light was now glinting in, shining through the chinks in my once impenetrable armour.

9
Eve's volcano

Although still troubled by frequent vulval flare-ups, I also sensed that my pain was becoming a gateway to something more. It seemed to be opening me up to experiences that spanned time and space, sleeping and waking, conscious and subconscious, which began to shift my awareness beyond the personal.

Nothing seemed to alleviate these flare-ups but time and patience, until the pain reset to the default white noise of low-level irritation. Burning soreness was still the primary symptom, in combination with episodes of stabbing pain and maddening itching and stinging. My bladder and urethral symptoms had also increased in frequency and severity, yet tests for urinary tract infections always came back negative, as did swabs for thrush and other infections. I was told by a urologist that I had a hypersensitive bladder, but vulvodynia was still the central diagnosis. Self-help measures and prescribed medication did little to manage the symptoms and nothing it seemed could provide long-term relief.

In spite of the pain, I still felt sexual desire; it had always been as crucial to self-expression as words, clothes, colour and paint. I craved touch, warm skin and a heart beating fast next to mine. I longed for the comfort of convention – a husband, a house, children and a scruffy dog – albeit with a little added zest and a twist. But the path to true love was a long and winding road pitted with potholes. I began a turbulent relationship with internet dating – land of eternal optimism and jaded resignation, of hopes, dreams, projection and rejection. They say it's a jungle out there, but who knew that would one day translate to headless Tarzan torsos on Tinder, and middle-aged men posing with a menagerie of wildlife, from dolphins to tigers to giant prize-winning carp.

How would I sell my unique combo of ME, vulval pain and welfare system chic to greatest effect? I had already tried and failed to 'go out' with Gareth, but at least if I met up with someone local I could get a subsidised cab home from a brief and sedentary date, long before the strike of midnight, avoiding my inevitable metamorphosis into a comatose pumpkin.

Several promising liaisons began with a flurry of enthusiasm, but ended in tears once my limitations became frustratingly apparent. I had begun seeing – in exhausting short bursts – a hot music producer who had a mixing desk that resembled the flight deck of an intergalactic space cruiser. One night, at his recording studio, we made a drunken and overly optimistic attempt at PiV – the buzz of behaving like a well person for a couple of hours had made me feel overly optimistic about my sexual capabilities.

The sex was uncomfortable but just about tolerable. Afterwards though, the burning soreness flared up and refused to calm down. Instead, the symptoms intensified and persisted for days and then weeks. I tried everything I had in my treatment arsenal, but nothing helped. Now I understood how some of the women in the support group had felt back in '94, who experienced unremitting pain 24/7. They looked crazed and weary, worn down by years of chronic symptoms that plagued them day and night, unable to get any relief despite trying all manner of treatments. I understood why they had lost all interest in sex, why they didn't think about it anymore, didn't want to read about it, watch it or talk about it, let alone participate. Right now, I thought, I would give anything just for a life without constant pain. That would be enough. Just to be able to pee, to shower, to sit without discomfort would be a gift, never mind erotic pleasure.

I curled up in a ball and sobbed. The burning, searing pain howled at me like a screaming banshee. It was as if the sweet, melting heat of sexual pleasure had been magnified and warped into a caustic, demonic means of torture. This was unlike other acute bouts of agony – toothache, severe period cramps or broken bones. The mother of all flare-ups, it refused to respond to painkillers, ice packs or desperate prayer. I cried out to God, to angels and ancestors, but no-one came to comfort me.

I lay awake for hours until suddenly something shifted. In the twilight world between waking and slumber, I felt a beautiful and calming presence – my daughter. I didn't know if I would ever hold her in my arms, or if she would ever find her way into the world through this burnt-out body, but I spoke to the promise of her. And in the early hours of the morning, the pain began to dissipate into a background hum as she sang me to sleep.

Two weeks later, in a hospital bed a few miles away, my sister-in-law endured long hours of labour, and after it was over she was blessed with a son – the first of our family's next generation. When I held him in my arms I felt wonder and joy, but also a deep hurt and silent rage at God, fate and my own body. This chronic pain, linked to my reproductive and sexual self, seemed to be open-ended and meaningless. I longed for labour, for pain imbued with hope and love; pain with a foreseeable end that would bring forth the gift of a new beginning.

If there was one thing I knew for certain growing up, it was that I would be a mother. I trusted in this one defining aspect of womanhood. I wondered about the specifics – the who, how and when – but I had faith that it would all fall into place. The life force that I had felt in the woods that flowed through creativity, blood, pain, sex and love would bring my baby forth. I trusted in this completely when everything else seemed hopeless. In the grand scheme of my life, giving birth felt as inevitable as my own death, but now – as I listened to the 'tick tick' of my biological clock – the wondering at times gave way to unease; the devil was in the details.

As well as this longing for a child, I also began to feel a deep sense of connection with my ancestors. Their sexual experiences, good and bad, had literally made my life possible. I carried their genes and felt a Darwinian sense of responsibility in continuing their journey – daughters becoming mothers, mothers becoming grandmothers – a daisy chain of DNA, adorning the passing centuries like a fertility garland. How would I feel if I was the ill-fated broken link in this evolutionary chain? As a childless spinster, I would be diverting their epic journey through the millennia into a dead-end cul-de-sac.

This growing sense of connection with my ancestors sparked a broader interest in the history of women's sexual health and emancipation. Three thousand years ago, the Ancient Greeks had some very dubious ideas about the female reproductive system. Hippocrates, known as the "father of medicine", and other physicians of the time, believed that the womb (uterus) could move around freely within a woman's body, causing all sorts of physical and psychological disturbances. On its travels, the "wandering womb" would supposedly press against other organs and nerves, causing health problems from convulsions to suffocation. They also coined the term "hysteria" from the Greek word *hystera,* meaning uterus. Hysteria symptoms could include anxiety, fainting, nervousness and a multitude of other complaints.

Treatment involved physical manipulation of the abdomen and the use of sweet and foul-smelling odours which were applied to different parts of the body. The aim was to try and attract or repel the womb, coaxing it back into its correct position. This bizarre concept persisted in various guises through the Middle Ages and far beyond.

To understand how cultural attitudes towards women's sexuality developed, we also need to look at early readings of religious texts. Take the biblical tales of the two Marys – the Virgin Mother of Christ and the reformed prostitute Mary Magdalene, Jesus' companion. For millennia, women were caught in the dichotomy between idealised virgin and stigmatised whore. Either pure and sexless, or lust-fuelled and in need of redemption. This binary left little room for manoeuvre. Women were often portrayed as dangerous temptresses capable of leading men astray. Consequently, women's sexuality was viewed as something that needed to be curtailed and the responsibility lay primarily with women – to dispel the male gaze by covering up, rather than with men to avoid temptation. A handy disclaimer for any man struggling to keep his libido and moral compass in check.

Before the Marys made their mark, Eve was the Old Testament's favourite naked pin-up, notorious for her role in the 'fall of man'. Tempted by the serpent to eat forbidden fruit – from the Tree of the Knowledge of Good and Evil – she persuaded Adam to take a bite. God then banished them from paradise and they and their offspring were doomed to a life of toil and struggle.

Remarkably, literal interpretations of Genesis still abound, with Eve and womankind continuing to cop the blame for all of man's afflictions. During my period of spiritual seeking, I once attended an Alpha meeting, attracted by the lure of free lasagne, profiteroles and crazed certainty. (Alpha is an eight-week evangelistic access course on the basics of Christianity.) The profiteroles were heavenly, if overly rich, rather like the chipper twenty-somethings who passed around the bibles and handbooks after dinner. One young woman, with waist-length blonde tresses, lamented that "Eve had let us down", but the good news was that we women now had a chance to try and make amends by using "our wits not our wiles" to make the world a better place.

Long before the creation myth in Genesis came Lilith, Adam's first wife. Lilith was ditched from the Canonical bible, perhaps to spare Adam any further indignity beyond the apple incident. I imagine his first marriage was hushed up in a 'what happens in Vegas, stays in Vegas'[1] kind of way by the bible's all-male board of editors. Adam's red-hot ex is notorious, though, in Jewish folklore for her feisty attitude towards male dominance. The story goes that when Adam tried to force her to lie beneath him during sex, she was having none of it; she believed they had been created equal from the dust of the earth and refused to give in to what she considered to be male dominance. Instead, she ran away to the Red Sea where she had sex with demons who were apparently way better lovers with a variety of hot tricks up their sleeves.

These attitudes to women's sexuality had an enduring effect, and in Medieval Europe midwives and wise women who managed women's sexual health were often accused of being witches. The *Malleus Maleficarum*, first published in 1487, was a comprehensive guide for the identification, prosecution and punishment of witches, written by two Dominican monks and inquisitors[2]. Accused witches could be forcibly searched for further bodily signs of guilt. Inquisitors would seek out the 'devil's teat' – an extra nipple or a raised bump somewhere on the body which was supposedly used by the witch's creature companion to suckle. This was often thought to be found in a hidden place, hence the clitoris was sometimes identified by male witch hunters as proof of guilt.

During the Victorian era, the clitoris was still a cause for concern within the male medical establishment, and "female hysteria" was back in the mix. Some doctors performed clitoridectomies in an attempt to 'cure' women of everything from anxiety to fainting fits and masturbation. Others adopted a different approach known as "hysterical paroxysm", which was essentially a medicalised form of orgasm using pelvic massage. As this was time-consuming for physicians, the vibrator was invented as a medical device to induce paroxysm in women diagnosed with hysteria[3]. Unlike the discreet bullet vibrators of today, the first electromechanical vibrator was a large, noisy and cumbersome machine invented for use specifically in medical settings. Essentially, this practice was medicalised sexual assault, but as Victorian alternatives go, preferable to having your clitoris surgically removed.

In the early 1900s, Sigmund Freud, known as the father of modern psychoanalysis, introduced his controversial ideas about female sexuality[4]. Again, the clitoris was viewed as problematic. Freud declared that clitoral orgasms were inferior to those that occurred during vaginal intercourse and that as a woman matures, her sexual focus should shift from the clitoris to the vagina. He considered orgasms achieved through clitoral stimulation to be immature and typical of young girls, whereas a vaginal orgasm was the mature form of female sexual pleasure (available primarily through penetration by a penis). He also suggested that girls' psychosexual development included a phase of "penis envy", leading to a sense of lack and inferiority. (We now recognise the complexity and individuality of female sexual experiences, and it is widely accepted that both clitoral and vaginal orgasms are valid forms of sexual pleasure for women.)

My interest in the history of women's health also led me to ask my mother about her own experiences and those of my grandmothers. As mentioned previously, my paternal grandmother died of cervical cancer when I was four years old, long before the introduction of a nationwide cervical screening programme in 1988. The symptoms she endured and the radium treatment prescribed were brutal.

Grandma, my maternal grandmother, was the queen of puddings. Throughout my childhood, her Sunday specials – Yorkshire pudding, raspberry trifle and cream slices – were a welcome distraction from a dull, impending Monday. Grandma's greenhouse was warm and fragrant with ripening tomatoes, her borders full of sweet peas, their heady scent now the essence of nostalgia. I'd had no idea about the darker episodes of her life; to me she had always been the quiet saviour of Sundays. However, through talking with Mum, I now had a glimpse into the health issues she lived through. Whilst giving birth to Mum, she had been "ripped to shreds" during a botched delivery, and the trauma, both physical and emotional, meant she was unable to get pregnant again for five years. With the onset of menopause, she had struggled with debilitating depression and stayed in bed for days on end, unable to function. Years later, she told Mum that she had overheard the visiting GP talking to my grandfather at the bottom of the stairs, telling him that she would have to be admitted to a mental asylum if she couldn't "pull herself together". Terrified, she dragged herself down to the kitchen and started baking – her only form of therapy in the absence of HRT.

Then there was Esther, another family member on my mother's side. As a young woman during the 1920s, Esther was in service at a large country house. Whilst working there she became pregnant; the circumstances were kept secret and the father was never revealed. Apparently, after the baby was born, Esther barely spoke again and fell into a deep depression that she never fully recovered from. The child, a daughter, was brought up by Esther's parents as if she were theirs – another sibling in their large family – to avoid the shame of Esther having a child out of wedlock.

Delve into any family's history and you are likely to find tales of suffering, oppression and shame in relation to women's sexual and reproductive health. There is a deep wound in the female psyche that continues to bleed, yet we also live in an era where a profound healing is possible – between the archetypes of masculine and feminine, between men and women, and among women themselves.

I began to sense the energy of the women who had lived before me – rising up and pooling like the magma cauldron of a volcano on the brink of eruption. I had always been fascinated by volcanoes; this molten, primal force that erupts at will from the core of our planet is uncontrollable and destructive, yet also possesses the transformative power to create an entirely new landscape. In my twenties, I hiked part-way up Mount Etna in Sicily – one of Italy's active volcanoes – frustrated that I didn't have the energy to make it all the way to its smoking peak. I also visited Pompeii and was awestruck by the casts of its Roman inhabitants, caught in the path of the erupting Mount Vesuvius. Those who had not fled the city were engulfed by the pyroclastic flow and then calcified by layers of ash, the form of their bodies preserved in action. Famously, there are casts of two figures locked in an embrace, apparently seeking solace in their last brief moments before being consumed by the volcano[5].

I imagined Eve rising up from the mythic core of Genesis, along with Lilith her kick-ass predecessor, and the billions of women who have walked the earth – virgins, wives, 'witches' and 'whores'; their power and potential a melting pot, flowing up through the rock of ages and erupting in an outpouring of pain, turmoil, wisdom and inspiration, to create the fertile ground of a new earth.

My experience of female pain in this broader sense continued to deepen, culminating a few weeks later in another late-night flare-up of vulval burning. The onset seemed frustratingly arbitrary, the pain arising without any obvious trigger. I lay awake in tears, but this time something had shifted – my pain was connecting me in a very visceral sense with the suffering of the women who had lived before me, and the women and girls today whose lives are still bound by oppression and ignorance. I felt them standing with me – their presence was palpable – and I also drew inspiration from their tremendous collective strength.

I had experienced both the pain and the pleasure of my sexuality and in that moment, it felt like a gift. I lived in a free country where gender parity was high on the agenda; I could explore my sexuality and creativity; I had access to modern medicine and emotional support; I could speak up, make my voice heard without shame or censorship, without risk of being labelled a hysteric, or burnt at the stake. I had the chance to do what the constraints of their era, or culture, had made impossible for them. What an incredible privilege.

Perhaps my health and limited resources were a barrier to effecting large-scale global change, but I knew I could at least speak up and make a difference on my own doorstep. The next morning, I relaunched the London Vulval Pain Support Group (LVPSG) that had fizzled in the '90s. Now, with access to home internet, Google, email and chat forums, it would be easier to connect and communicate with women on a citywide scale. As well as offering a safe place to vent, I was determined that our pain and frustration would inspire positive action. We might be living in the shadow of Eve's volcano, but it was on fertile ground.

10

The 'Chilli Pepper Sex' club

The LVPSG relaunched one Saturday morning in my living room with eight women, two pots of tea and a multi-pack of McVitie's. I had been in touch with Kay and Juliette (their real names), co-founders of the original support group back in the '90s, and Kay had sent out an invitation to those on the original 'snail mail' list, which had resulted in our group of eight. Kay was a trustee of national charity The Vulval Pain Society (VPS) and the kick-ass queen of vulval activism.

We sent posters advertising the group to sexual health clinics across the city and set up a webpage and chat forum. It was 2002, and with home access to the internet (which had been lacking back in the early '90s) our membership began to grow; eventually we had upwards of 200 women signed up to our online forum. My living room couldn't contain us beyond the first couple of meetings, but I discovered the church at the end of my street had a hall and meeting rooms for rent at low cost. We met there every six weeks for a couple of hours, each making a small donation to cover expenses. Between 10 and 25 women turned up to each meeting, with up to 100 at larger workshops and events. I was still battling chronic fatigue, and chairing the sessions would wipe me out for days, but running the group gave me a sense of purpose and momentum that outweighed the fallout.

A series of framed prints adorned the entrance hall to the church building, depicting various biblical events. I searched for Moses and the burning bush, but disappointingly he was nowhere to be found. In the Old Testament story, the bush is on fire, yet not consumed by the flames – a rather fitting analogy for living with vulval pain. Moses may have been omitted from the lineup, but the venue was now host to a posse of burning bushes, and we were doing our damnedest not to let ours consume us.

During the summer, building work needed to be carried out, which meant there would be no access to the hall or meeting rooms. Instead, we were offered use of the church itself. I felt an unexpected pang of conscience – how would the congregation feel if they knew we were talking sex, lube and penis size in their conservatively-clad spiritual home? It wasn't as if we were planning to shoot porn or a Madonna-inspired pop promo from the pulpit, so why did I feel this odd sense of unease? I found myself making a guilty confession to Ethel, the eighty-something church warden. I had told her we were a women's health support group, but now I found myself flagging up possible "talk of a sexual nature" and the sharing of faulty-vagina monologues. I needn't have bothered; Ethel was unfazed.

"I don't think God will mind, dear," she responded. "He gave us [women] all one of those and must've known there might be problems so I think he would be understanding, especially while the building work is going on."

And so we lined the pews for Saturday service, passing

around free samples of organic lube and hypoallergenic wash cream before getting down to business. Discussing sex in church – albeit under the moniker of 'women's health' – felt awkward at first, provocative, amusing even, but also profoundly moving. Talking about our sexual pain in a place where, for centuries, sex and female wisdom had been off limits felt healing and empowering. It was an experience that would continue to resonate in other sacred spaces I visited.

Our shared discussions on sexual health were also a barometer for popular culture and the ever-evolving language of sex and anatomy. Most of us opted for medical terminology, and vagina and vulva, when talking about vulval pain; the terms felt neutral rather than loaded with cultural mishap, and it was clear whether we were talking 'inside' or 'out'. Though fanny, vag and minge entered the mix for emotional emphasis when vulva didn't feel up to the job.

In a colloquial sense, vagina is often widely used to refer to the whole shebang; vulva has come late to the party. But in recent years, the hoo-ha over anatomical incorrectness has escalated – so does being genitally PC really matter? From a feminist perspective, using vagina to refer to the female sex organs in their entirety has been viewed as problematic because it places emphasis only on the part that gives heterosexual men the most pleasure. It doesn't help that the basic meaning of the Latin word vagina is 'sheath', or 'scabbard for a sword', the passive receptacle for a weapon[1].

The Latin meaning of vulva is more benign – in a literal sense it means 'wrapper' and was used to refer to the womb, though subsequently it has come to mean the external female sex organs[2]. My favourite bit of gynae etymology, though, has to be clitoris, which is far less likely to rub anyone up the wrong way. Originating from the Greek kleitoris, one of its many possible roots is as a derivative of kleis, a key by which one gains entry to a door[3]; in other words, the access point to understanding female sexuality. Though the symbolism also works in a more literal sense – finding the key before attempting to enter the proverbial door should surely be mandatory 'Sex 101'. There's a 'knock-knock' joke in there somewhere.

The crux of the issue, in terms of this ever-evolving language, is of course about autonomy and respect. Women need to have authority over their bodies, sexual health and sexual pleasure. That means everyone needs a clear understanding of the female anatomy, and it's easier to do that if we're all on the same page of the anatomy textbook, and using the same terms. But while it is important to use correct terminology in certain contexts (medicine and education, for example), trying to police the ever-evolving language that weaves its way through sexuality is an impossible task and misses the point. The richness and variety of etymology around sex is not only inevitable but crucial to cultural dynamics – it is when medicine and education intersect with creativity, art and erotica that innovation happens. This merging of information, language and sub-cultures creates friction and impact, drawing people into a conversation they might otherwise not engage with.

Jamie McCartney is a Brighton-based sculptor, and creator of what was formerly known as The Great Wall of Vagina, which was first exhibited in 2011. (The title referenced The Great Wall of China, with 'vagina' and 'China' a rhyming play on words.) However, the eight-metre wall sculpture is in fact made up of 400 plaster casts of vulvas, all of them unique. The women who participated in the project were between the ages of eighteen and seventy-six. Included are mothers and daughters, identical twins, trans men and women, and women pre and postnatal and pre and post labiaplasty[4].

McCartney has since renamed the project The Great Wall of Vulva, after feedback from women's groups over the years pointing out that the title was anatomically incorrect. Does artistic licence trump political and anatomical correctness? Perhaps, but along the way the artwork has become an international educational initiative, on display in numerous countries worldwide, and if it's aiming to promote clarity over confusion, then it's vulvas all the way. Unfortunately though, 'vulva' doesn't rhyme with 'China'. I suppose McCartney could always reimagine the work as a Vulva Revolver – the plaster casts exhibited on a revolving turntable, like a giant kebab.

When it comes to the appropriate use of sexual language, the benchmark is surely context and intention. It's all about who is using the term, the intention driving the language, and the context in which it is delivered and understood. On a gynae couch, it might be *vulva* and *vagina*, but on the phone to a friend, or in a lover's arms, it might well be *vag*, *pussy*, *minge* or *vajajay* – for all-inclusive ease. Or, if you're feeling emboldened, the controversial c-word might even get an outing. To reduce the risk of this book being dumped in online publishing's 'filth bin' with assorted porn and erotica, and removed from general searches, I've been advised to give the c-word the 'star' treatment. Supposedly, roving AI bots like to seek out mentions of 'C U Next Tuesday' resulting in punitive consequences. So, here goes. Long before c**t became a paragon of offence, it was used in a sacred context in reference to the Hindu fertility goddess Kunti, the great Yoni of the Universe. It has since evolved through the Latin, Old Norse and Germanic languages and is linked etymologically to words such as country, kin and cunning[5]. The word is also the root for the Scots' *ken*, relating to knowledge, and *cunctipotent*, meaning all-powerful – still listed in the English dictionary and surely due for a comeback. However, during the Middle Ages the term became associated with obscenity and insult. The Christian clergy used the term 'devilish c**ts' to refer to matriarchal pagan shrines such as caves and holy wells, and the word became synonymous with 'witches' and female cunning.

The c-word carries the weight of centuries of misogyny and insult-hurling, but is now being reclaimed by some feminists as a powerful and positive expression of the female form. Still, it remains a loaded term and I don't recall anyone at the support group ever giving it a shot. Well, perhaps in occasional reference to an arrogant and unprofessional clinician, but not as a genital descriptor.

Our meetings then, at the corner church, were conducted with language that was mostly medical, sometimes colloquial, and always alive with emotion. It was important to create a supportive environment in which we could each vent our feelings and be heard, but we were also keen to create a positive sense of momentum, and to use our pain and frustration as impetus for action; to raise awareness of vulval pain with the medical community, media and public, and among sexual partners and patients themselves; to push for research and new treatment options, and to ensure that as many women as possible had access to the best care.

Although our experiences were various, certain themes emerged that would recur again and again – not being believed ("it's all in your head"), problems getting a correct diagnosis and accessing effective multidisciplinary treatment, not feeling like a 'real' woman and resulting low self-esteem, and secrecy and shame around the issue. We all agreed on one thing – we needed a revolution in care and treatment options, and in how the media and popular culture engaged with women's sexual health.

Women from all walks of life turned up at the door, from eighteen to eighty. For many, vulval pain had taken a devastating toll on their relationships, ability to work, self-esteem and mental health, but there were also stories of victories small and large, of joyous episodes of pain-free sex, longed-for pregnancies, respite and recovery.

Although the group's focus was on vulvodynia as a primary cause of vulval pain (and that was what the majority had been diagnosed with), many of us also had to contend with other sexual health issues as an added complication. For example, vaginal thrush and bacterial vaginosis, skin conditions (eczema and lichen sclerosus), menopausal atrophy, pelvic floor dysfunction, STI, urinary tract issues, low libido and vaginismus.

Frustratingly, the long-term prevalence of one condition might be a factor in kicking off another (for example, the chronic pain of vulvodynia may trigger secondary vaginismus and psychosexual issues). Or a course of treatment might inadvertently exacerbate a secondary issue (supposedly, using steroid cream regularly for lichen sclerosus (LS) can thin the skin, dampen the immune response and make vaginal thrush more likely to develop). Trying to interpret and treat vulval symptoms such as burning pain, rawness, itching, aching, prickling and stabbing sensations when there is more than one vulval issue in the mix can make long-term management of vulval pain a minefield. Symptoms are often attributed to one issue only, meaning that other important parts of the puzzle are ignored and dismissed, or the treatment offered is limited. Successful management is often a jigsaw of pieces – a vulval pain syndrome rather than a single issue with one neat, tick-box treatment. A multi-disciplinary, multi-treatment approach is now considered to be the optimal way forward, with various approaches running in parallel. These might include specialist pelvic floor physiotherapy and use of dilators, medication, psychosexual counselling, and holistic therapies. For many women, this approach to care can be difficult to access as funding, expertise and treatment choices vary hugely across regional and clinical settings.

To address this issue, one of the key aims of the VPS and LVPSG was to educate medical professionals about vulval pain – from a medical standpoint, but also from the patient's perspective. We produced an information leaflet for women to take to their doctors, gave talks and presentations to medical students, midwives, GPs and gynaecologists, and even lobbied parliament about awareness and funding of women's sexual health services. The LVPSG has organised regular workshops and talks on specific aspects of vulval pain management (with guest speakers including doctors, psychologists and sex toy instructors), and continues to run webinars online covering similar themes, in order to reach a wider audience. I also began building links with women's health organisations and minority communities – an Islamic women's group and the LBGTQ+ community – to raise awareness of vulval pain in specific contexts and to encourage collaboration.

Another of our objectives was to support and inform women's sexual partners about vulval pain. Several key themes would recur at our meetings: What's the best way to discuss vulval pain with a new partner? Can you have a fulfilling sexual relationship without penetrative sex? What defines *real* sex anyway and who decides what's 'normal'? How can you prevent sexual health issues affecting the dynamics of a relationship? It felt important that we addressed these issues, not only within the context of the group, but also from a partner perspective, so we invited partners along to specific workshops and speaker events. It is not unusual for some men to experience erectile dysfunction in response to their partners' vulval symptoms, due to concern and misplaced guilt. And new partners, often uninformed about the issue's pathology, may wrongly interpret vulval pain as a critique of their sexual technique or a lack of attraction.

Recent research has shown that partner responses are crucial to the successful management of vulval pain[6]. Looking at a continuum of partner styles – with anxious, overly kind and concerned male partners at one end of the spectrum, and negative and even hostile types at the other – a study found that both extremes may be detrimental in the everyday sexual lives of women with vulvodynia. Whereas facilitative partner responses – being caring and encouraging – may improve sexual functioning.

The LVPSG would continue to thrive, with some members finding the group's online chat forum a more accessible way of connecting, along with attending intermittent workshops and speaker-led events. Other regional support groups popped up around the UK, all of us under the umbrella of the national Vulval Pain Society. In effect, we were part of an international 'club' that includes millions of women worldwide, many of whom – as a result of isolation and misdiagnosis – are unaware they are members.

Years later, my partner at the time gave the support group a nickname – a wry nod to the burning of vulvodynia. I'd been working with my friend and colleague Sabine Tyvainen on a short film to raise awareness of the condition, and we were using a sliced pepper on a barbecue to represent a burning vulva. The Women4Real film went viral on YouTube[7].

One Saturday morning, as I headed out to a group event, he bid me goodbye with a grin.

"Hope all goes well at the 'Chilli Pepper Sex' club."

His quip became my go-to moniker for all of us who burn – and throb and hurt and sting. Together, we're fired up to find a solution.

The Chilli Pepper Sex Club was my original title for this book, but I was advised that having 'Sex Club' emblazoned across the front cover could be problematic if I hoped to avoid banishment to the afore-mentioned 'filth bin'. Such are the perils of self-publishing. After fuming at this annoyance for weeks, I reluctantly decided to remove 'Sex' from the title – in an attempt to get the book through the publishing process and available to a general audience. If you're reading this, hopefully I've succeeded and you found my work in the memoir section rather than sandwiched between *Laced with Lust* and *Mrs Maquire's Dirty Secret*.

11
Long lost lips

Papilloma De Vere and Chlamydia Addington Jones. I imagined they ran a PR company together, out of Papilloma's townhouse in Kensington.

I was sitting in a vulval clinic waiting room during the summer of 2005, rifling through sexual health leaflets to pass the time. The names Papilloma and Chlamydia sounded rather upmarket, whereas Herpes and Gonorrhoea might have been the titles of Old Testament warmongers; they had a gravity to them that smacked of biblical wrath.

On the wall opposite, an A4 poster asked if I would consider organ donation in the event of my untimely death. I lost myself in a sci-fi fantasy where genital transplants were possible and visualised the perfectly functioning *Playboy* pussy I'd have transplanted in place of my own. As I flicked through the pages of a tattered *Hello* magazine, I guessed at which celebrity versions – hidden beneath red-carpet frocks – might be a good prospect for transplantation. Gwyneth Paltrow's appealed. I imagined it smooth and perfect, airbrushed like her flawless complexion.

I'd seen a documentary once about a transplant patient who had apparently taken on the personality traits and characteristics of the donor. The man had a new heart and lungs and claimed he now had unexplained cravings for quarter-pounders and meat-laden fried breakfasts, when prior to the operation he'd been a vegetarian. I might wake up post-op with someone else's vulva and a taste for liquorice and Brussels sprouts. Perhaps I'd acquire the donor's sexual appetite as well and develop a kink for toe-sucking, head-to-toe latex, or…Chris Martin, and vegan cupcakes.

I was jolted back to reality by the sound of my name being called by a nurse. I followed her into a consulting room. On the side table there was a 3D-model of the female reproductive system. As I sat there studying it, I realised I didn't really want someone else's vagina – I was quite attached to my own, if only it would work properly.

I was here to see a vulval specialist I'd heard great things about via the LVPSG, who would become my go-to gynae expert over the next fifteen years. At a previous appointment, she had suggested that along with vulvodynia I was exhibiting signs of LS, a long-term skin condition that can cause chronic itching and soreness; it affects both men and women and can occur on any part of the body, but more often affects the vulva, the foreskin of the penis and the anal area. Today, using a colposcope to get a magnified view, she was going to look at my vulva again and take a biopsy to confirm the diagnosis.

Lichen sclerosus can cause white patches to appear on the vulval skin which, without treatment, can become thin, fragile and prone to minute splits and fissures. The vulva may even scar and shrink over time, leading to a loss of the labia minora (the inner folds of vulval skin). This shrinkage can narrow the entrance to the vagina, making sex painful as a result. The condition is estimated to affect around 3 per cent of the female population, is more prevalent in Caucasians, and is most likely caused by an overactivity of the immune system[1]. As with vulvodynia, it cannot be transmitted to a partner as it is not an infection. Lichen sclerosus is incurable and in a small number of cases can lead to vulval cancer, but more often periods of remission are possible if it is diagnosed in its early stages, and symptoms can be managed with steroid cream to calm the immune response.

Of course, I had googled visuals of lichen sclerosus soon after my new doc mentioned it. In Google's 'haunted house' of sexual health jump scares – warts, blisters, oozing discharge and parasitic infection – LS was a pale, ghostly apparition with open lesions for eyes, leaping out of the laptop, wailing like Munch's iconic painting, *The Scream*. I scrolled through graphic photos of severe, untreated symptoms – open sores, vulval skin cancer and large patches of wrinkled, discoloured flesh. In comparison with this terrifying dermatological apocalypse, vulvodynia's 'invisibility' seemed politely innocuous.

In the colposcopy suite I was ushered onto the examination table, feet in stirrups. My gynaecologist strode in.

"Are you okay if a couple of medical students sit in for educational purposes?" she ventured.

"Of course," I replied, trying to sound blasé. "The more doctors that know about this condition the better."

But beneath the self-assured veneer I felt uneasy, particularly when I discovered one of them was drop-dead gorgeous and could've walked straight off the set of ER. I wanted men like him to find me sexually alluring, not view me as a grim medical specimen.

The nurse aimed a spotlight between my legs and my gynaecologist pointed a video camera in the same direction, instructing one of the medical students to turn a large video monitor towards me so that I could see the screen.

"This is our new edition to the gynaecology suite," she said, "so you can see what's going on, if you want to."

Suddenly my vulva was a TV star. It filled the screen, stage struck and unready for its 15 minutes of fame. The showbiz pussies I'd seen previously in boyfriend-imported porn videos were Brazilian-waxed, sexual superstars. But this was no porn flick – it was a horror movie. I'd trimmed and shaped my bikini line especially for the occasion, but magnified at this resolution, my handiwork was an ugly mass of bumpy hair follicles. The audience of five moved in for a better view; I was convinced I saw the *ER* doc squirming.

Seeing my vulva magnified to such a monster size, all the fears, myths and emotions associated with it were magnified too. I remembered a book I'd read about ancient cultures that viewed the vagina as a misplaced mouth, with deadly teeth known as vagina dentata. If my vagina were a mouth, what would it have to say?

The scene from *Alien* flashed through my head, where the screeching alien baby bursts out of John Hurt's stomach. I imagined a creature screaming banshee-like from my vagina, voicing the pain and frustration that had gestated there over the years.

I could feel tears welling up – the nurse handed me a tissue, the audience looked uncomfortable. My doctor made a stab at gynae-inspired humour:

"There's definitely evidence of mild LS, but don't worry, steroids will sort it out, and not the kind that will make you look like Arnold Schwarzenegger."

I managed a smile – I liked her. She was by far the

best vulval specialist I'd encountered on my journey so far and she knew when to make me smile and when to get serious.

Fortunately, despite having had LS for some years (my inner labia showed signs of fusing and shrinkage) there were no large areas of pale skin or other obvious giveaways that might out me to a 'layman' on the dating scene. That's what was going through my head as the medical students looked on – never mind how my vulva felt or malfunctioned as a result of LS, just so long as it still *looked* 'normal'. Men were turned on primarily by visual stimuli – it was a 'truth' I had absorbed through decades of cultural osmosis; to be 'good enough' I must live up to a specifically defined vision of the female form, and thanks to the porn industry, that now included aspirational "vulval architecture".

My gynaecologist had used this rather grandiose phrase in reference to my minimal labia minora. From then on, whenever I watched *Grand Designs* on Channel 4, presenter Kevin McCloud's architectural spiel would have distinctly vulval undertones. Substitute vulvas for buildings and McCloud's insights are sublime: "Some of the most exciting [vulvas], the finest [vulvas] on this planet, have had difficult histories, difficult births"[2]. They most certainly have.

An hour after my vulva's TV debut, I sat in a café over the road waiting for a lift home. Suddenly, one of the medical students rushed in, grabbed a coffee and a Danish, and gave me a cursory smile of recognition. I imagined mine was one of many ailing vulvas he'd seen that day in high resolution; perhaps he'd be relaying the highlights of the 'freaky fanny' show in the pub later over a pint and a packet of pork scratchings.

I was frustrated. It had taken years to get the vulvodynia diagnosis and to adapt to living with the condition, so did that diagnosis still stand, or had LS been the real culprit all along? And why had it not been picked up by a doctor earlier, given there was evidence I'd had symptoms for some time? I had been given mild steroid creams over the years for my "sensitive skin", but LS had never been offered as a diagnosis by any of the sexual health professionals I had consulted, and I had seen forty or more since the age of fifteen.

How is it possible for serious gynaecological conditions such as vulvodynia and LS – which can have such a devastating impact – to go undiagnosed for so long? It's something I hear time and again from so many women with vulval symptoms. Clinicians and GPs need to be able to identify LS and vulvodynia in their early stages, and to deliver effective treatment using a multidisciplinary approach. Education is crucial, yet these conditions barely get a mention in most medical school curriculums.

My gynaecologist explained that in my case it was more useful to view my symptoms as a vulval pain syndrome that was multi-faceted, rather than narrow the diagnosis to one label only. Yes, vulvodynia was still in the mix (jangling neuropathic pain), along with overactive pelvic floor muscles and recurrent thrush, which 'skin scrape' tests showed I still had at a chronic low level.

Occasionally I'd have flare-ups of thrush with an obvious vaginal discharge, but often soreness and itching were the primary symptoms; the candida was causing an inflammatory response in my vulval skin and this wouldn't show up on standard vaginal swabs. Itching and soreness are also characteristic of LS, and the soreness and burning of vulvodynia could also mimic thrush, so

I would find it tricky at times to know what was going on and which treatment to opt for.

My GP certainly had no idea – it was all guess work based on previous tests and diagnoses – and the local sexual health clinic could only treat symptoms that tested positive for infection. Only my gynaecologist had the breadth of knowledge to manage these conditions effectively, but as an NHS patient, I could only see her every nine months to a year. And only ongoing because I had LS, which was considered to be a disease that needed monitoring because of the small cancer risk.

I would need to treat each issue specifically, but also adopt a holistic approach to manage the multiple systems in my body that had a part to play. My nervous system, psychological and emotional state, gut microbiome, immune response, and muscle tone were all contributing to a 'feedback loop' that was influencing the symptoms.

A multi-faceted approach would be crucial in months to come. I was fortunate in being able to access a range of services via the vulval clinic including pelvic floor physiotherapy, psychosexual counselling and specialist medical care. But for many women, diagnosis and treatment of vulval conditions is a lottery – in the UK the standard, consistency and breadth of care available varies widely, as does collaboration between hospital departments and community clinical services. Currently, the majority of vulval clinics in the UK only offer women with vulvodynia or LS two appointments before discharging them back to GP care. Lack of NHS funding for women's sexual health services means millions of women are not able to see a specialist consultant ongoing.

The strong steroid ointment I'd been given to treat the LS worked quickly and effectively to dampen the itching and soreness, but I had to make sure I didn't use it too often as overuse of topical steroids can thin the skin and encourage thrush.

Outing myself as having LS felt like a very different prospect to doing so with vulvodynia. Neither condition is transmittable, so there was no sense of responsibility around fessing up, though I needed to offer an explanation, at least to long-term partners, as to why penetrative sex was painful. Vulvodynia's lack of visible symptoms had been frustrating at times, particularly in terms of convincing doctors of its existence, but this gave it a reassuringly benign feel when I did choose to talk about it to partners. Everything looked A-okay down there, so I could keep up appearances, even if my nerve endings were jangling below the surface.

If a prospective boyfriend googled vulvodynia there would be no visual jump scares; LS on the other hand, jeez. Okay, my vulva could pass as normal – ironically I'd even had compliments from sexual partners on its minimal aesthetic – but I didn't want 'Munch's vulval scream' flashing through a guy's head when he went down on me. I decided that in a sexual context, LS would be alluded to vaguely as "sensitive skin", with vulvodynia the star of the show.

Perhaps I should have been brave enough to name it rather than shame it, but the prospect felt overwhelming. It was difficult enough explaining to a prospective partner that I couldn't have 'normal' sex without pain. The idea that I might also declare a skin disorder – one which could alter the 'normal' appearance of my vulva – was terrifying, even if these skin changes were masquerading as culturally admired minimalist architecture.

Navigating your way through the dating world when

you have a sexual health issue can be a minefield. How much detail should we give new sexual partners upfront? And what do we expect them to share with us before we jump into bed? It's certainly something I've thought about over the years – what to say, and when. Clearly, if it's a condition that's sexually transmittable then it's about ethics and integrity, and taking responsibility for protecting your partner. Though these can be murky waters: what if you're non-symptomatic, using barrier contraception, and haven't had a flare-up for decades, *and* you're taking suppressive medication – for herpes, for example? Or you have non-symptomatic HPV which affects up to 80 per cent of the population anyway? Must everything be declared in full before the first sexual encounter? Ideally yes, but in the real world, getting real isn't always as straightforward as we would want it to be.

When to divulge an STI is also a question that has legal implications, though this aspect of disclosure is unlikely to play on the minds of most. Prosecutions for knowingly passing on a "serious" STI are rare and remain controversial, but have nonetheless been the subject of tabloid debate and outrage among STI stakeholder groups. In 2011, a British man, David Golding, was prosecuted for grievous bodily harm after infecting his girlfriend with the herpes virus. It was the first time someone in the UK had been imprisoned for spreading herpes and he received a 14-month jail sentence[3]. Prior to this case, there have also been prosecutions in the UK for passing on HIV and Hepatitis B. However, it is not always straightforward to determine grounds for guilt in these cases as a state of "recklessness" must be proved on the part of the perpetrator. And what counts as a "serious" STI has not been determined by law[4].Given the UK's catastrophic problem with prison overcrowding and a stretched legal system, it seems unlikely that the Crown Prosecution Service will be prioritising the policing of our sex lives any time soon.

If a sexual health condition is not transmissible, does it matter when you disclose it? If it's something that flares up regularly and can affect sexual functioning, does a potential long-term partner deserve to know from the get-go? Occasionally, getting a perfunctory sexual experience under my belt before the big declaration has boosted my self-confidence, though mostly at the expense of my own physical comfort and pleasure if I've been feeling sore. More often, speaking up before we're actually between the sheets has been helpful, and I'm fortunate that the majority of my partners have been understanding and empathetic. I've tried to be clear, concise and positive in my delivery and flagged up that I still enjoy sex, just not penetration when my pain flares up.

Tone and timing have certainly played a big part in how I've delivered the message over the years, and how it's been received. And so has understanding and communicating that sex isn't just about function and performing 'the act'; it's an opportunity to get creative, explore and build intimacy – physical and emotional. I need to think about my partner's physical and emotional wellbeing but also my own, and that's a balance that can be tricky to strike.

While we ought to be able to talk openly about sexual health, sex and desire refuse to be politically correct. Getting too graphic about your condition with a new partner just before you get it on can kill the mood in an instant. But then again, sometimes being honest in the moment, with positivity, can feel empowering, and confidence is an attractive quality. It depends on who you're with, how you're feeling and how you present the issue.

Sometimes I've drip-fed a new partner the basics and filled in the details of my diagnoses further down the line. And even then I've condensed disclosure into what I deem to be manageable headlines rather than an in-depth news report. But there have also been instances when I've told someone in full on the first date about my vulval pain because I've felt comfortable enough to do so.

Further along in a relationship, I've also struggled with how much to reveal about my symptoms and how often to deliver an update. Whilst I don't want to share my vulva's every gripe and groan with my partner, it would feel inauthentic to slap on a smile and pretend I'm not in pain. Finding a middle ground has meant developing trust, empathy and mutual understanding.

Disclosure is a personal thing, but sharing my LS status has certainly felt different to talking about vulvodynia, and different still from mentioning thrush, or my run-in with HPV.

Soon after my LS diagnosis, my upstairs neighbour Jude gave me a goodbye gift, as he prepared to head off to LA to live with his American girlfriend. He appeared at my front door with a large cardboard box full of VHS video tapes – his porn stash. Jude knew I was interested in sexual health issues and thought I might like the porn "for research…and stuff".

His transatlantic girlfriend worked in the movie industry and I imagined she had a stylish, minimalist house in the Hills, and a stripped-back Hollywood bikini line to match. I remembered a slogan I'd once seen on a greetings card – it was beneath a cartoon of a woman in a floaty dress. She was stepping out of a beautician's salon on to a breezy street: 'She went in for a Brazilian and came out with a chilly'un'. Greetings card gold.

Jude's cardboard box, I soon discovered, was full of 'chilly'uns'. I pulled the curtains and pressed play.

12

Houston, we have a problem

I sat slumped on the sofa in my living room, my finger hovering over the mute button, in case new neighbours Doug and Sarah arrived home through the communal front door. From Brazilian pool parties and Californian condos to a tired London flat in need of Kevin McCloud's design input – Jude's VHS collection was a global pornucopia.

Why was I watching this? I wasn't sure. Out of curiosity? As a turn-on? For "research…and stuff" as Jude had suggested? Some of it turned me on; some of it didn't. Some of it probably shouldn't have, but sexual kinks and quirks are immune to political correctness. Still, did I really want to be watching other people have vigorous penetrative sex – the Olympics of sexual prowess – when I couldn't even manage an average pain-free shag? I also felt uneasy about the ethics of porn, but my ambivalence didn't stop me pressing play.

"How does porn make you feel?" I remember the workshop leader posing the question at an online women's event I had signed up to a couple of years earlier. "Think about how comfortable you feel with porn. Does it make you feel empowered and curious, or shocked and uncomfortable?"

What about 'horny', I remember thinking, isn't that its primary objective? Porn made me feel all of these things and more – sometimes in isolation, sometimes all at once.

As I slid my hand into my jeans during *Sadie's Hot-Dogging Drive-in*[1], my mind also began to wander. I wanted to know more about Sadie as a whole person, rather than just a 'hole' person. I found myself wondering about her home décor, the contents of her fridge, and her relationship with her parents. But this intrusive musing soon subsided. As I binge-watched my way through Jude's porn, the people getting it on eventually became 'white noise' – an indistinct commotion that masked any underlying traces of personality.

The focus of the experience became about the scenario and the power dynamic; the energy of the encounter rather than the idiosyncrasies of those taking part. I began to fast forward through the banal setups and stilted dialogue and used shorter clips for quick results; I hadn't anticipated getting this involved, but I was starting to get the hang of it, this porn thing.

(My second-hand porn habit wasn't something my mother had anticipated either. A couple of years later, whilst looking for an old recipe book, she would discover *Sadie's Hot-Dogging Drive-in* in a cardboard box full of porn videos – in amongst an assortment of junk I was storing in her garage pending a flat move. That was an awkward conversation.)

At first, I had found it difficult to watch all this pounding and grinding – the 'real' sex that I was missing out on – but inadvertently it became a strange kind of therapy. My brain had processed so much PiV that porn had become the equivalent of a Paul McKenna self-hypnosis course. For a while at least, I had become desensitised.

Watching sex no longer hurt, even if doing it still did. A few choice clips were guaranteed to turn me on time and again, but I soon felt numb to most of it. Disturbingly, I had also become numb to the ethics of it. I chose not to think about the wellbeing of the women involved and only watched softcore clips that were relatively benign. But I couldn't shake the images of some of the more aggressive stuff I'd viewed. I began to think more seriously about porn's exploitative and misogynistic underbelly – the circumstances under which some of it was made and the effects of consuming it.

A recent study suggests that 42 per cent of internet users view porn regularly and the global porn industry is estimated to be worth over $97 billion[2]. The same research indicates that 64 per cent of young people aged thirteen to twenty-four actively seek out pornography weekly or more often, and a staggering 88.2 per cent of scenes in porn videos contain acts of physical aggression. The relationship between pornography, misogyny and male violence continues to be widely debated. A UK Government literature review on the issue acknowledged that a direct causal link can be difficult to establish as human behaviour is influenced by numerous interrelated variables and subconscious factors. However, across all of the methodologies reviewed, substantial evidence was found of "an association between the use of pornography and harmful sexual attitudes and behaviours towards women"[3].

Of course, everyone has their sexual proclivities and between consenting adults particular dynamics can fuel creativity, trust and intimacy. But when certain behaviours are perpetuated as sexual norms and viewed indiscriminately and habitually, it is bound to shape the perceptions of those watching. Global estimates vary on porn usage, but a 2023 study that looked at visits to the popular website Pornhub indicated that almost 80 per cent of visitors were men and 20 per cent of those watching were women. Almost half of those visiting the site were between eighteen and thirty-four[4].

Porn is now ubiquitous – available globally at the click of a computer mouse. Decades ago it required back-street stealth or brazenly reaching for the top shelf in the newsagent's and was, officially at least, an eighteen-plus pursuit. Though I first encountered it at a much younger age. My best friend and I found some ripped pages from a rather niche porn magazine on the common behind her house. I was ten years old. A naked blonde woman, with large breasts, was pictured getting creative with half a pound of butter and a drawer full of kitchen utensils, including a wooden spoon and a non-stick frying pan – the images are stuck in my head for all eternity.

I remember feeling aghast at what she was getting up to, and confused. There was a sense of excitement at having discovered something forbidden, but the overriding feelings were of fear and shame. I'd caught glimpses of 'dirty mags' on the top shelf at the newsagent's and heard about the dodgy men who bought them – pervs and 'flashers' who wore brown macs and emerged from the bushes to expose themselves to women and kids on recreation grounds.

I felt uneasy about the gaze that might have fallen on the ripped page before mine; the fingers that might've torn the woman from the magazine. We knew he was out there somewhere, this faceless man who had ripped the woman from the centrefold. Now she would be carried across the dark, dank common on the gusting wind until the paper she existed on disintegrated into the mud. For many years after the discovery, the image of her spreadeagled on the page would randomly emerge from memory and I'd feel an uneasy array of emotions which I couldn't articulate.

When I was around thirteen, a small tattered photo of a guy with a huge erection was doing the rounds at my girls' school. We giggled nervously, concerned that we might one day be confronted with something of similar proportions. Sex loomed large on the horizon.

And in my early twenties, I remember buying the newly-launched For Women magazine and the awkwardness I felt as I handed over my cash at the counter. In my eagerness to dive in, I thumbed through it in an empty lift as I headed up to the ticket hall at Goodge Street tube station. Sadly, the new magazine wasn't the liberating, lust-fuelled experience I was hoping for. It was full of oiled-up hairless beefcakes, their faces blank and gormless, and the articles were mind-numbing to match.

I was in my thirties before I discovered Nancy Friday's erotic short stories for women and the swathe of erotic fiction written by female authors. As for 'live action', free access porn sites didn't kick off until the early noughties, with YouPorn launching in 2006. It would be years, though, before porn made for women by women got into a groove and the likes of video director Erika Lust cornered the market.

After bingeing on Jude's porn for a month, I was bored. My own imagination was much better equipped at turning me on than the banality of most of it, and there was no sour aftertaste. I'd had my fill of super-sized cocks and doll-like hairless, lipless pussies, and trowelled on slap. My feelings about porn continue to evolve – the relationship between ethics and sexual desire is tricky to navigate.

The summer I received Jude's box of porn, I also watched a TV documentary about the new trend for 'designer vaginas'. It was gruesome viewing, but strangely compulsive. I watched transfixed as a surgeon known as 'Dr Designer Vagina' performed a labiaplasty operation which involved plenty of slicing and sewing with the intention of reducing the size of the patient's inner labia (genital lips).

The camera cut to a shot of a motel pool, softly lit. A woman with giant, inflated breasts emerged naked and dripping and recounted a tale so fantastic I almost choked on my Doritos. This was Houston, an American porn star who had undergone "labia-reduction surgery". Apparently, at her request, the procedure had been filmed for her fans and distributed to subscribers via the internet. The three pieces of labia were encased in acrylic on a marble stand and reportedly sold online via an erotic auction site. The bizarre piece of 'sculpture' was reputedly bought for $50,000 by porn king Dennis Hof, owner of the Moonlight Bunny Ranch, a licensed brothel in Nevada[5].

I tapped her name into Google and a profile piece popped up – a New York Observer article from 2000.

"I wanted smaller pussy lips," she said by way of explanation for the surgery[6].

Apparently, Houston had made around 200 films and once held the world gang bang record for having sex with 620 men in eight hours. A sexual superstar, she had reaped the rewards of porn stardom. Wasn't she just living out her own XXX version of the American dream? Houston's labiaplasty had apparently improved her sexual functioning and her porn prospects – enhancing her "look" for those all-important close ups.

A labial nip'n'tuck was all the rage in Hollywood and the procedure was making its way to the UK. Women wanted fashionable 'porn pussies' – neat and trim. And the trend for pubic hair removal meant more and more vulvas were now being exposed to scrutiny.

Interestingly, research has shown that when labiaplasties are sought for aesthetic reasons, there is no difference in labial dimensions between women seeking and not seeking the procedure[7]. In other words, it's not size that matters, but the weight of meaning women place upon it – the result of cultural perceptions about what a perfect vulva should look like. Still, we live in a culture where facelifts, boob jobs and Botox are mainstream. And I was willing to shave my legs, dye my hair and shave my bikini line. Wasn't having your labia reduced just a few rungs up the ladder from a Brazilian wax?

I couldn't convince myself. "Houston, we have a problem..." The infamous quote from the Apollo 13 moon mission flashed through my brain. I knew several women at the LVPSG who had undergone procedures on the vulva for medical reasons which had resulted in scar tissue formation and nerve damage. There were also emerging reports in the media of some women experiencing either chronic pain or lack of sexual sensation after botched labiaplasty operations.

Take Laura's story, for example. I happened to see her post in an online chatroom, and she has given me permission to quote some of her comments here using a pseudonym. Laura was just fifteen years old when she had the operation, which was carried out by a private physician in the UK. She was feeling "vulnerable and body dysmorphic" and had requested the procedure for cosmetic reasons, but the consequences were devastating.

"I didn't have a concept of the difference in vulvas or their beauty," she explains. "Doctors didn't tell me any different and thought it acceptable to completely amputate [my labia minora]. They robbed me of my joy and pleasure and replaced it with constant pain and burning, and an aching heart."

Relationships, "intimate and ordinary", have been difficult to maintain since, says Laura, as she feels traumatised by the experience. Understandably, she feels angry that she was allowed to undergo such a serious medical procedure at fifteen without being properly informed about the diversity of normal female anatomy – or the risks involved.

"I'm thirty now and there's not a day gone by where it hasn't affected me one way or another," she adds. "It's taken this long to be able to fully talk about it."

It's important to point out that there may also be practical, rather than aesthetic, reasons why some women seek labiaplasties. For example, if they're experiencing irritation and pain during exercise or sex as a consequence of having large, protruding inner labia. Or if they have experienced trauma or damage to the labia during childbirth. The procedure is only likely to be of benefit, though, if the inner labia are larger than 4 cm and causing significant chafing and soreness[7].

Proponents of labiaplasty get tetchy when a parallel is drawn between the procedure and the disturbing practice of Female Genital Mutilation (FGM), but you can see why without clinical need the 'designer vagina' might be viewed as a westernised nod in the same direction; a dubious cultural practice that in some instances can do real and lasting damage to women's bodies.

Current guidance from the Royal College of Gynaecologists states that no-one under the age of eighteen should have a labiaplasty because the labia can continue to grow from puberty into early adulthood. And, as in Laura's case, the impact of cultural influences at a young age is a barrier to informed consent. Labiaplasty is rarely available on the NHS and most procedures are now carried out in the private sector under strict guidelines.

Female Genital Mutilation is a criminal offence in many countries, including the UK. It comprises all procedures that cut and or otherwise injure the female genitals for non-medical reasons. Surgeons performing labiaplasties for aesthetic reasons risk breaching the FGM law if they remove too much tissue or operate on the clitoral hood, which some women request be removed if it is hanging down.

Typically, FGM, also known as female circumcision, is carried out on girls in infancy and before the age of fifteen as part of a cultural rite of passage upon entering womanhood. The practice is common among African communities in central, eastern and western Africa, though it also occurs in the Middle East and some Asian countries. Although the procedure has been illegal in the UK since 1985, there is also evidence to suggest it still occurs here.

As part of the practice, the clitoris and parts of the labia may be removed, often using a razor blade or broken glass in rural African communities, and in some cases the two sides of the vulva will be stitched together. This may be done using thorns or thread so that a bridge of scar tissue forms over the entrance to the vagina, leaving only a tiny opening.

The World Health Organization estimates that 200 million girls and women alive today have undergone FGM. At current rates, an additional estimated 68 million girls face being cut by 2030[8]. As you might imagine, the consequences of the procedure can be devastating – severe pain, haemorrhaging, infections, psychological trauma and major problems with menstruation, sex and childbirth are common. It is estimated that almost a third of girls subjected to the procedure will die as a result.

Organisations such as Amnesty International are campaigning to end the custom, but communities that practise FGM claim it is an important part of their culture and tradition. Perversely, it is often women who perpetuate FGM. Older, respected women frequently carry out the procedure (without any form of anaesthetic) because doing so validates their social standing in the community. A girl who does not undergo FGM in a community where it is held in high regard is likely to be shunned and considered unfit for marriage.

We might sneer at these barbaric practices living in our westernised 'bubble', but are we not also victims of our culture? We may have a head start on human rights and live in a society that extols personal freedom, but ultimately our choices are dictated by our culture, just as they are in every country worldwide. An exciting sex life and fashionable genitals are now an aspirational commodity. Mercifully, we are not being held down screaming and being cut with a dirty razor blade, but we are being brainwashed by magazine and internet images that persuade us to hand over vast sums of money to go under the knife.

The trend for 'designer vaginas' also got me thinking about women like me who were living with the skin disease LS. I remembered one young woman in the LVPSG telling us that her labia had shrunk as a result of having LS long term. She had been devastated at the changes in her anatomy (and had a tough time managing the infernal itching and fragile skin) but her new sexual partner, as yet unaware of her skin condition, had complimented her on her neat and tidy "porn pussy". He didn't like "meaty lips" and she had "nothing hanging out" he said. She may have been battling a chronic skin disease, but she ticked the "porn pussy" box and was his idea of 'normal'.

When it comes to vulval architecture, the reality and diversity of 'normal' is of course vast. If you're in any doubt, just google the afore-mentioned Great Wall of Vulva or check out similar projects that have been created since. Yet the trend continues to be for porn-inspired, doll-like genitalia that is closer to that of a pre-pubescent girl than a grown woman.

"It looks cleaner, feels better and you can see what's going on," according to a twenty-something guy on another TV show I watched.

It was a strange irony that while women with LS were distressed at losing their labia to disease, others were busy handing over their cash to have theirs removed in the name of sexual allure. Of course, choosing to 'sculpt' your genitals for cosmetic enhancement (or medical reasons) is vastly different to the pain and mutilation that is inflicted through disease or violence. Like everything in the sexual realm, consent is paramount. But who is really making the decisions here? We like to think we're making empowered choices, but more often than not it's cultural pressures that drive us – a female aesthetic sold to us by the internet, fashion, media and porn: to feel good enough, we must look a certain way, despite the long-term health implications.

Along with the labia and clitoris, the hymen is another feature of vulval architecture that has long been a cause of controversy. Misconceptions about the hymen – particularly in relation to virginity – are still widespread. Rather like the appendix, the hymen is not thought to serve any specific physiological function, though it has been suggested that it may help to protect the vagina from bacterial infection during infancy[9].

Contrary to urban myth, a torn hymen won't grow back as a result of abstaining from sex for a lengthy period, and claims that an intact hymen can be used to determine virginity are nonsense. A sexual partner can't assess a woman's virginity by looking, as hymens come in a variety of shapes and sizes – and there may not be blood on the sheets either. Tampon use, sports activities and general 'wear and tear' growing up can stretch the hymen, so it is common for women not to bleed when first having penetrative sex. (If blood spotting does occur, it may be down to a torn hymen, but equally it could be caused by overly vigorous first-time sex – lack of arousal and lubrication can cause small tears in the vulval and vaginal tissue.)

'Virginity tests' and hymen reconstructive surgeries prior to marriage continue to take place in some countries and cultures. In 2018, the UN Office of the High Commissioner for Human Rights, WHO and UN Women called for a ban on 'virginity testing' as this humiliating and traumatic practice can have devastating consequences for the women and girls involved[10].

Vulval architecture has become a property market, and it seems fitting that I return to property show presenter Kevin McCloud for the final word. Or to be precise, a few words from one of his art and design critic predecessors, the Victorian social thinker John Ruskin.

There has been much speculation about Ruskin's sexuality and he was rumoured to be repulsed by women's pubic hair and menstrual blood[11]. Some biographers claim Ruskin's only experience of the female nude was admiring Greek statues and paintings lacking pubic hair, and that the reality of a real woman was too shocking to contemplate; his marriage was unconsummated and annulled soon after.

Speaking to Grand Designs magazine, McCloud paraphrases Ruskin's views on great buildings: "Architecture should also speak of its time and of its place…of the people that use it and commissioned it"[12].

I'm sure Ruskin would be thrilled to know that his insights can also be applied rather brilliantly to vulvas. From pubic grooming and vajazzling to 'designer vaginas', disease and FGM, vulval architecture speaks of our time, and of the people who use and possess women's bodies – men, media, porn, big pharma, and women themselves.

As with all great architecture, beyond aesthetics we need to focus on functionality and sustainability, and how it all works as a whole. I was starting to realise that I was more than the sum of my hole, though my vagina had been pretty life-defining so far.

13

The floor keeps the score

Porn may have numbed me to the sting of seeing other people have sex, but it was only a short-term fix. It still hurt like hell to do it for real, and the NHS continued to be tasked with fixing the mechanics of my vulval pain.

Fortunately, my gynaecologist believed in a multidisciplinary approach to treatment and her vulval clinic worked in liaison with the hospital's psychosexual team and women's health physiotherapy unit. Along with using a topical steroid to manage the LS, I was referred to these services to address the vulvodynia.

Psychosexual therapy was offered to help me untangle the emotional fallout of living with vulval pain. And I had physiotherapy to retrain my pelvic floor muscles, which had become tight from unconsciously clenching up in response to long-term pain.

"Just because this is 'psycho' therapy, it doesn't mean I think you're imagining your pain."

That was one of the first things Kate, my psychosexual counsellor, said to me at our first session. Hearing her acknowledge that was huge. Ten years previously, I'd had doctors telling me I should just "relax and have a glass of wine before intercourse"; it was "all in my head" and would "probably go away on its own". Kate understood that vulval pain was a medically-recognised condition, and that it had affected my life in significant ways.

We talked about goals for our sessions together and decided that one aim would be to reduce the negative impact of some of my thoughts and beliefs about the pain, and about myself. We explored what it meant to be a 'real' woman, a phrase that had looped around in my head for years. For me, being a 'real' woman meant fulfilling my sexual and reproductive potential. In short, being gloriously average – pleasurable PiV sex, marriage and motherhood, a successful career and a mortgage. These were my markers for happiness – tangible, physical expressions of success in the world at large. But what would success look like at a deeper level? How would it *feel*? We talked about courage and resilience, love, creativity and compassion, and how these attributes might also be markers for a life well lived. Though at thirty-four, I would happily have welcomed pain-free sex, a husband and a baby over nebulous inner wisdom. But surely it was possible to have it all? That was the promise being sold in the ads for tampons, takeaway coffee and incontinence pads that peppered my favourite TV shows.

We also talked about "outercourse" as an important aspect of sexual connection as well as intercourse, and about "performance" versus real intimacy. I explained that PiV was everywhere – in novels, movies and porn it's the default setting for heterosexual interaction. In Jude's porn, in Hollywood movies and in the many novels I'd read, when sex was featured it was PiV for the most part. Absorbing all this pop culture shagging, when you're unable to have penetrative sex without pain, can put a serious dent in your self-esteem. Penetration somehow equates with depth of intimacy, depth of connection, depth of worth. It's depicted as the pinnacle of a heterosexual encounter, with non-penetrative sexual practices and other sexual behaviours relegated to foreplay or kink. But it wasn't just the cultural norms that factored into my feelings around PiV sex; it felt like an instinctive need to have my partner inside me and to do what my body was built to do. Kate made a valiant attempt to persuade me otherwise, but I could never quite shake the notion that 'real' sex was PiV.

Along with psychosexual counselling, Kate suggested some practical breathing exercises and visualisations to help calm my nervous system. I found the "physiological sigh" to be a useful tool – taking a deep breath in through the nose, a further short inhale, then exhaling fully through the mouth. I still do five of these breaths in succession multiple times throughout my day to calm my nervous system and relax my pelvic floor. When it comes to guided visualisation exercises though, I'm easily put off by distracting details – the 'wrong' kind of new age muzak, trite scenario or vexing voice can have me reaching for the stop button, or my imagination will provide an escape route:

At a yoga class I used to attend regularly, the instructor would often bang on about dolphins and sunsets at the end of the session as part of a "relaxing guided meditation". Or reel out her favourite, a mystical journey on a magic carpet: "Imagine you're flying across the desert sands until you reach a colourful spice market next to an oasis – the scents waft upwards, it smells divine and you feel a deep sense of peace…"

Suddenly, I'm flanked by two Iraqi fighter jets and forced to dive and land my magic carpet in the market below which has turned into the set of Homeland. I'm wielding a pistol alongside Carrie Mathison as we tackle a terrorist bomb threat…

"And open your eyes and relax. Namaste."

As we rolled up our yoga mats to leave the class, the women around me appeared super-chilled. One regular commented on how relaxed she felt after class meditations which she looked forward to every week. I wondered why my brain wasn't wired liked hers – guided visualisations of this type always fire up my neural pathways rather than calm them down.

The practice of mindfulness has proved to be more beneficial, and is quite different to guided visualisations and relaxation techniques. It requires focused attention – consistently bringing the mind back to the present moment – whereas relaxation often involves daydreaming and mind chatter. Our minds are continually flitting between the past and the future, often with judgement and worry, and the practice of mindfulness breaks this cycle.

Mindfulness can also reduce pain signals in the brain whereas, unsurprisingly, chronic stress and anxiety can amplify them. The practice dates back around 2,500 years to eastern philosophy and the dawn of Buddhism. More recently, its secular spin-off has been touted by self-styled course leaders and online apps as an antidote to the stress and strain of modern living. But although mindfulness has become a popular buzzword, its benefits are scientifically proven, and mindfulness-based cognitive behavioural therapy (MBCT) has had encouraging results in the treatment of provoked vulvodynia. A Canadian study showed that MBCT led to lasting improvements in symptoms of pain intensity and sexual distress, and an increase in self-compassion[1].

Everyday activities such as walking, eating and cleaning your teeth can all be carried out mindfully – by being fully present to the bodily sensations that arise, rather than succumbing to the usual inner commentary we all have going on. Meditation is also a way of developing a mindfulness practice in which the breath, a mantra, a focal point, or repetitive movements of the body (such as walking, yoga or tai chi) are used to anchor the wandering mind in the present moment.

I've had an on-off relationship with mindfulness and meditation for decades. In my early forties I lived in a retreat centre for three years where daily meditation was central to the ethos and I've also worked at a Buddhist school, but my practice still waxes and wanes. At times, mindfulness has worked wonders for me – after just a short session, it's as though my brain has been jet-washed and my thought processing suddenly feels refreshed and crystal clear; I've also experienced a reduction in pain levels. But it can also be an uncomfortable experience that releases tightly held emotions. When I attempt to meditate with my eyes closed I can feel overwhelmed by my overactive imagination, particularly if I'm feeling anxious, upset or in pain. Instead, I find that meditation with an open focus works best – my gaze gently focused on a point in the middle distance whilst also sensing the feeling of space around me. Sometimes, if I'm in pain or feeling emotionally wobbly, I find that shorter pauses throughout the day are more manageable than a lengthy, one-off session that can feel too intense. A mindfulness practice that involves gentle repetitive movements such as yoga, tai chi or walking can also feel more beneficial.

It takes me out of my head and focuses my awareness on my breathing and on the flow of energy through my body.

Contrary to popular opinion, not all approaches to mindfulness are of equal benefit to everyone – it's important to find ways of practising that suit individual needs. Mindfulness can be a positive and powerful tool, but proceed with caution if you have chronic pain, depression, anxiety or a neurodivergent condition such as ADHD and are new to the practice. Stopping to fully check in with your body and mind may, in some instances, cause an influx of thoughts and emotions to arise, which can trigger anxiety. You might want to start with support from a qualified MBCT clinician who knows their stuff.

Thankfully, Kate understood some of these pitfalls and was able to utilise mindfulness, relaxation exercises and talk therapy to help me untangle my vulval pain in the context of my daily life, relationships and self-esteem. It helped to have somewhere to go and vent my frustration and to implement a mindfulness practice at home to help manage stress and pain. It was the ongoing mutual support, though, from other women with vulval pain, via the LVPSG, that really made the difference. And it was pelvic floor physiotherapy – physical exercises with breathing and deep relaxation – that would kick-start my recovery.

Women's health physiotherapy is a growing area of specialty that treats a range of conditions relating to the pelvic floor that affect the bladder, vagina and bowel. The pelvic floor is a hammock-like set of muscles that run from the pubic bone at the front to the tailbone at the back. Pregnancy and postnatal issues are a focus, but so are painful bladder syndrome, vaginismus and vulvodynia. It's all about treating pelvic floor muscles that have become underactive or overactive – too loose or too tight.

After childbirth, the pelvic floor muscles can become stretched, weak and lengthened (underactive) and the emphasis is on toning them up. Kegel exercises (clenching and releasing the pelvic floor muscles) can help with incontinence issues and vaginal tone. At the other extreme, overactive muscles are often a feature of vulval pain and overactive bladder syndromes. In the same way that some people will, often unconsciously, hold all their tension in their neck or shoulders – and go on to develop headaches as a result – a similar process goes on in the pelvis. Overactivity of the pelvic floor muscles can occur gradually, or as the result of a trigger within the body – a flare-up of vaginal thrush, for example, which causes vulval discomfort.

In an overactive pelvic floor, the muscles are working harder than they need to, which means they gradually shorten and become stiff and tense. This reduces blood flow which causes impaired tissue oxygenation and a build-up of lactic acid, resulting in sensations of burning, aching and rawness. It's a cycle that is worsened by anxiety which can make us clench the pelvic floor as a protective response to discomfort, often without even realising it. The nerves in the area become sensitised and the muscles become tight and painful (tension myalgia).

Physiotherapy approaches to treating vulval pain have changed over the two decades I've been dipping in and out of sessions. Initially, biofeedback was in vogue, then it was all about releasing "trigger points" high up inside the vagina. More recently, the focus has been on gentle pressure and massage just inside the vestibule.

The terms 'hypertonic' and 'hypotonic' have been used to describe muscles that are either too tight or too loose, respectively. But 'overactive' or 'underactive' are the terms now used more commonly to refer to muscle tone.

I was diagnosed with an overactive pelvic floor at my first physio session. My physiotherapist was an absolute star. She needed to insert an egg-shaped vaginal probe to measure my muscle tone and somehow managed to do it without a massive "ouch" from me. I felt sore, but once it was in place it hurt less. And it was worth the discomfort as I could now see an electronic read-out on the computer screen next to me, which provided a visual representation of what my muscles were doing (biofeedback).

My resting tone was way tighter than the normal muscular resting level indicative of a healthy pelvic floor. My physio directed me in a breathing technique that involved relaxing down into my pelvis on an out breath. To establish a normal resting tone, I found I needed to gently bear down with my pelvic floor muscles rather than try and relax.

I had to continue to do the exercises regularly at home and she also gave me a set of vaginal dilators to use. They were conical white plastic, moulded in five sizes from 'fore finger' to 'hung like a horse', with a grey screw-on handle. The idea was to gradually increase my tolerance level from small to large, while relaxing at home.

It felt rather clinical lying on my bed – day in, day out – inserting a chunk of plastic without a sexual context. Sometimes I'd fire up my imagination and get turned on which helped things along. Though the jury's out on whether using sexual arousal as part of the process jangles the nerves with too much stimulus, when the object of the exercise is to reduce pain signals. More often, I'd leave one in while I reclined on the sofa and watched *10 Years Younger*, or waited 'on hold' to customer services while they attempted to fix my latest consumer glitch. Getting out of my head and distracting myself helped me relax into it.

It was a gradual process over many months and one I would return to over the years if my pelvic floor got too tight and sore. If I stopped doing the exercises for more than a month or so I would find that the pain increased again. Now and again I'd get impatient and try and push forward too quickly, gung ho, with a larger dilator, only to trigger more pain and sensitivity. A bout of thrush, stress and anxiety, or an attempt at sex might also kick off the pain and I'd have to wait until things calmed down then slowly build up my tolerance again.

Years later, I was also taught "trigger point release" to relieve muscle tension higher up in the vagina. This could be done using fingers, a dilator or a specially designed 'pelvic wand' to put pressure on specific points and relieve muscle tension from inside. Exploring my vagina was challenging; although I was becoming more comfortable with inserting the dilators, feeling around inside my body with my fingers felt unsettling. Pressing on painful 'trigger points' often released tightly-held emotions along with the muscle tension. When I poked around inside this vulnerable part of myself it was like prodding at hidden sore spots in my psyche.

In recent years, when I've been for treatment, the physiotherapist has used her thumb to put gentle pressure on the muscles just inside the entrance to the vagina. I've also used this technique at home and found it effective in reducing pain, but only if I continue the practice daily. Women's physiotherapy continues to evolve and trends and practices also vary among practitioners.

Having had an ambivalent relationship with vaginal penetration for so long, it took time to build my confidence and to trust that these practices wouldn't worsen the pain. I needed a change in mindset – to view my vagina as a potential space that could gently expand and adapt rather than a dark, rigid tunnel of doom. Tentatively, I began to think of it as a more comfortable space that I might eventually welcome someone into – a relaxed chill-out lounge rather than a throbbing nightclub rammed with troublemakers on the brink of brawl.

Penetration is a powerful word. Google its meaning and you're likely to encounter the terms 'pierce', 'puncture' and 'probe'. Penetration is "an impelling force or compelling power that achieves entrance"[2]. It is about entering with force rather than being invited in. "You could talk about the penetration of a jacket by a knife, or the penetration of a fortress by an army"[3].

In a consensual context (and in possession of a resilient, fully functional vagina) being 'taken' hard might feel sexually exciting, but not when vulval pain is in the picture. I needed to retrain my brain and my nervous system to think of my vagina as a safe space rather than a danger zone. That meant gently encouraging my vagina to invite the dilator in rather than ramming it through the proverbial door.

Over time my muscle tone began to get closer to a normal resting level. It was like going to the gym – as long as I kept up the exercises I began to see positive results. "Are you still going to the 'quim gym'?" a friend at the support group once asked me with a grin. Like the infamous c-word, 'quim' is slang for vulva or vagina and apparently off limits because of its misogynistic history. The word play made me smile though, and why not reclaim it for positive use? The term is a possible derivative of *queem*, meaning pleasure, but it may also have its roots in the words *cwem* (women, wife, queen) or *cwm* (Welsh for 'valley')[4].

While I'm on a roll about women's physiotherapy, it's worth mentioning here the relationship between an overactive pelvic floor and vaginismus. Increasingly, women with symptoms of vulval pain are being diagnosed with an overactive pelvic floor. This may generate pain further up in the vagina, the bladder and related areas, whereas vaginismus refers only to the muscles at the lower third of the vagina. Women's health physiotherapy can help treat both conditions – using dilators, breathing exercises and other techniques.

Vaginismus is a mind-body response to the fear of vaginal penetration – the muscles at the entrance to the vagina tighten involuntarily, clamping up and making penetration impossible or very painful. Rather than being a precise diagnosis, vaginismus is now more often referred to as a clinical syndrome that includes converging issues – pain, anxiety, overactive pelvic floor muscles and problems enabling penetration[5].

Women with vaginismus may describe the sensation of a physical block when they try to insert something vaginally. That's different to overactive pelvic floor muscles that may be in a constant, chronic state of increased tension a lot of the time.

For some women with vaginismus, the debilitating symptoms have been ever present – from puberty and attempted use of tampons to painful first experiences of sex (primary vaginismus). Vaginismus can also occur, though, after vaginal function has been normal for many years (secondary vaginismus). It can be total or partial – the latter refers to some penetration being possible, but often with accompanying pain. Vaginismus can also occur intermittently in certain contexts and circumstances only.

Pelvic floor physiotherapy explains women's physiology in clinical terms, but 'tight' is a word loaded with cultural meaning. Throughout history the tension between 'loose' and 'tight' has been hanging in the balance when it comes to women's sexuality.

For centuries, women were viewed as highly-strung hysterics whose emotions could spring loose at any time, and with a dangerous sexuality that could tempt men off the straight and narrow. Hence they needed to be controlled by the patriarchy – constricted by rules and laws, corseted so they could hardly breathe, and yet amenable and open for sex on demand.

Today, the pressure is on to tighten up "muffin tops" and maximise "thigh gaps" through sit-ups, squats and spin classes (or plastic surgery and liposuction if you're looking for a shortcut). The bar for sexual desirability is set by spray-tanned Instagram influencers with washboard stomachs and toned curves, who've been waxed to oblivion.

And it's not just abs and thighs that need toning – a tight, but not too tight, vagina is the goal. Too tight and sex will likely be painful and something to avoid – the old misogynist insult 'frigid' is still doing the rounds. But loosen up and enjoy your sexuality and you're also on dangerous ground. Historically, 'loose woman' was a derogatory term that implied sexual promiscuity and loose morals. And as for childbirth, woe betide you skimp on your Kegels afterwards; there's a plethora of online insults available to describe your 'loose' vag.

And then of course there's menopause. Is your dry, shrinking vagina feeling too tight? Are you feeling "uptight"? Or perhaps, paradoxically, you're "losing your grip". These are the half-truths and beliefs our colloquialisms have bound us up in. Too tight, or too loose? As a woman, it's hard to win.

14

One more try

Thanks to pelvic floor physiotherapy, I was making progress at last in managing my vulval pain. However, CFS (or ME) was still curtailing my attempts to get out into the world and meet a long-term partner. I had just turned thirty-five and my biological clock was ticking ever louder.

My symptoms were just as debilitating as when I had crashed out of work six years ago. Still, I pushed myself to host LVPSG meetings regularly, and got a cab to a sedentary internet-inspired date now and again, relying on the adrenalin rush to make it through before crashing out exhausted the next day. But I couldn't work at a computer for longer than half an hour or I'd get a blinding headache and brain fog would set in. And walking even a short distance would make my legs feel leaden, and the grinding fatigue would kick in.

I wanted to get back to work, to get on the property ladder, to get on a plane and see the world. But still unfit to work, I was reliant on welfare benefits and had tried every possible avenue to get well. Or so I thought.

One day a friend mentioned reverse therapy (RT) – an approach to managing CFS that she had read about online[1]. So called because it claims to reverse symptoms and attitudes to the syndrome. Initially, I dismissed it as yet another woo-woo 'cure', but when I read up on it the central premise made sense.

I'll state upfront that RT has never been subjected to the rigour of clinical trials. It has never been endorsed by the medical community or CFS organisations, and has often been dismissed as placebo effect – or as a way of managing symptoms (in a similar way to cognitive behavioural therapy) rather than fully explaining their true cause. While it works brilliantly for some, completely alleviating symptoms and transforming their lives, others find it difficult to implement and it is less effective.

Years later, I mentioned my experience of RT in an article I wrote for a medical publication. The trolling I received on social media from the hardline CFS community was vicious, and I'll admit I thought twice about discussing it here. But keeping my head below the parapet to avoid the snipers and not acknowledging the experience I had helps no-one.

Whatever your degree of scepticism, to dismiss my experience is to discard a piece of the puzzle of this syndrome that destroys so many lives. We need to look at the onset and recovery experiences of a broad range of people with CFS and understand the correlations, and take into account the complex physiology that manifests this condition. Only then will we find a treatment that works effectively for all.

Reverse therapy asserts that the symptoms of CFS are the complex result of interactions between mind, body, emotions and the environment. Symptoms are a manifestation of "bodily distress", which occurs when the limbic system – a complex system of nerves and networks in the brain – senses there is an emotional challenge that needs resolving. This leads to muscle tension, and a host of other debilitating symptoms that are frequently reported as part of CFS.

Reverse therapy is based on the notion that our intelligence can be split into two camps: 'headmind' is the thinking intellectual mind and 'bodymind' is the more intuitive sensory intelligence that arises from the body.

In his book *Reverse Therapy*, John Eaton (the therapy's founder) suggests that emotions such as fear, anger and sadness have a natural action cycle – "starting when bodymind registers that we first face a challenge, to completion of the actions it wants us to take to restore equilibrium"[2].

If we take no action then bodymind 'turns up the volume' on the emotion by activating the limbic system, resulting in physical symptoms which increase as time goes on. "Unresolved emotions create a build-up of tension which results in bodily distress, and the potential onset of illness."

The limbic system is rather like a radar station that monitors both our external environment and internal environment (thoughts, feelings, gut reactions, heart rate and so on). It also assesses how well our internal reactions are helping us to adapt to the environment we are in.

Reverse therapy asserts that symptoms are a form of intelligent communication. They result from bodymind activities that transfer information to and fro between the brain and the nervous system, immune system, muscles, skin, glands and gut. Symptoms are signals that something is wrong with your way of being. They can be seen as prompts for the question, "What is my body encouraging me to *do* about this feeling or situation?"[3]

In my case, bodymind could be asking me to speak up about how I really feel, or to let go of self-criticism and just do what is good enough, rather than trying to achieve perfection. These were two of my personal triggers, identified by Eaton during my first RT session with him.

Other people with CFS will have their own symptom messages, based on specific emotional triggers. Just as the body registers learning experiences through 'muscle memory' (such as learning to ride a bike) it also stores emotional memories – states which are reactivated when a similar situation is encountered. According to the RT approach, it is these emotional 'alarm reactions' that trigger debilitating physical symptoms.

As with riding a bike, the physiological mechanism by which the process happens does not manifest as conscious thought – it just happens. So we may not make the connection between stifled emotions and the resulting physical symptoms.

To restore health and balance, the key is to connect to bodymind, and to tune into the feelings and emotions that are arising during a period of distress just before the onset of symptoms. It is not enough to analyse the cause of the symptoms – bodymind requires immediate action to resolve the problem, so it doesn't need to trigger the alarm mechanisms which follow on from distress.

At my first session with Eaton, he asked me to talk about the life events that were occurring when my symptoms first started. We looked at the pressures I was encountering at the time and I was able to recall some of the feelings, sensations, emotions and thoughts that were coming up back then. This helped me to get a sense of what it was bodymind was trying to tell me through the symptoms at that time. Then we looked at what my body might be seeking now.

In my early teens I would feel frustration and rage rising whenever I felt my external world wasn't living up to my internal imaginings and expectations. I would try and try, and push harder and harder in an attempt to get the results I wanted. And I would push uncomfortable feelings of hurt, anger and even love down on a daily basis; they might be expressed through creative means, but rarely to the person or persons involved in the causation of the emotion.

Growing up, "just try your best, it doesn't matter how well you do" was meant as a loving reassurance, but somewhere along the line I warped the message into "try as hard as you possibly can to get it right, or you'll never feel good enough".

During our sessions, Eaton would point out again and again that I was trying to "bludgeon" my way through things instead of just moving through daily tasks at a moderate pace.

Trying mode continues to drive me to distraction. Often I'll realise that I am *trying* to do something, rather than just allowing myself to go with the flow. A few years ago, my close friend Sabine Tyvainen, a health psychologist, stuck sensors to my head and rigged me up to her neurofeedback software. She wanted to monitor my brainwaves during different states of activity as part of a research project she was undertaking about types of focus. It showed that while I thought I was meditating, I was actually *trying* hard to meditate. Instead of generating a calm alpha wave state, I had 'high alert' anxiety waves tearing through my brain as I tried to get it right for her project. As a reminder to chill out, I now have a Jedi quote from Yoda stuck to my fridge – "Do, or do not, there is no try".

I left my first session with Eaton armed with several personalised messages which he told me to start acting on in day-to-day situations that they applied to. For example, "my symptoms are here to tell me to stop pushing down my feelings and start speaking up about how I really feel NOW", and "my symptoms are here to tell me to stop trying to 'get it right' and to just do what is good enough NOW".

This felt uncomfortable at first – it's one thing to speak up and another to do it without coming across as a temperamental diva. Communicating with sensitivity and finesse takes practice, and reversing entrenched behaviours and thought patterns is a minefield. And doing without getting into an anxious trying mode has been a tough habit to break.

I awkwardly told a friend that the way she spoke to me felt patronising and judgemental and I wasn't going to take her advice, rather than just letting it slide; I did some writing and went with the flow instead of endlessly trying to perfect one paragraph; and I stopped walking towards an arbitrary point that I'd set myself as a limitation (the post box) which made me anxious, thinking that if I went further I'd push myself into a fatigue hangover.

The practice also meant striking a balance each day between 'have to' and 'want to'. When headmind is functioning in a healthy way it stimulates creativity, productivity and optimal decision-making. But headmind is often influenced by ego, and actions motivated by 'should', 'have to' and 'ought to', setting up a cycle of self-imposed judgement and fear.

Bodymind, on the other hand, is more interested in restoring balance to all systems of mind and body by encouraging activities that offer variety, joy and inspiration. It is looking for challenges to be overcome and emotional needs to be addressed, so resting all day is unlikely to reduce symptoms (though including rest and relaxation in daily activities is of course important for general wellbeing).

I had my doubts that this approach was going to reverse my symptoms entirely – I had been ill for so long and the fatigue and muscle pain felt so entrenched. But over time I was able to do more and increase my level of functioning. The aching, grinding fatigue was lifting. Remarkably, by acting in the moment as symptoms arose, they would reduce in severity. It was a kind of 'Pinocchio' effect – lie to myself about how I was really feeling (or what bodymind needed in that moment) and I would experience an immediate physical manifestation of that untruth.

Reverse therapy suggests that people get stuck in the illness loop by, understandably, becoming anxious about symptoms. The limbic system's 'radar' is then triggered and is constantly scanning for symptoms to detect the perceived level of threat. This creates more symptoms as bodymind notices the person is worrying about the symptoms rather than addressing the underlying message.

Eaton claims this may account for why people with CFS often associate a bout of fatigue with previous exertion (hours or days prior), when it is actually how they are feeling in the moment that has triggered the anxiety loop. I'm not entirely convinced by this facet of the theory, but it's an interesting concept. He also has a different view on the commonly held notion that a viral illness (such as glandular fever / Epstein-Barr) may be a cause of CFS.

At fifteen, when I had first experienced 'post-viral fatigue', it was assumed the symptoms were caused by the 'glandular fever-related virus' that preceded the onset. Glandular fever (infectious mononucleosis) is caused by the Epstein-Barr virus (EBV) – one of eight viruses in the herpes family and common in humans. Some studies estimate that 90 to 95 per cent of adults worldwide have been infected with EBV[4]. However, only 30 to 50 per cent of teens or young adults exposed to the virus are likely to develop symptomatic glandular fever[5].

Reverse therapy asserts that rather than the virus causing CFS, it is the limbic system triggering tension and anxiety that lowers immune function, allowing this and other viruses to take hold in those who are particularly susceptible to bodily distress.

Out in the world, armed with Eaton's message cards, it was often tricky trying to understand why a symptom had arisen, and what to do about it. I'd try too hard to work it out and get stuck in my head. Reverse therapy became yet another thing I was trying to get right. Sometimes it would drive Eaton nuts – his tone would become terse and he'd look quietly riled. He had a shaven head and resembled actor Donald Pleasance as Bond villain Blowfeld (minus the menacing facial scar). I once had a dream about him in his black swivel chair, cradling a white cat on his lap and feeding a pool full of piranhas. But he had a twinkle in his eye and when he was on form he was brilliant, helping me solve what was going on with perfect clarity. (Later, I would also have sessions with his female colleague – we were a similar age and she understood the anxiety generated by the 'tick tick' of my biological clock.)

Other people noticed that my health was improving and were keen to know why. I felt embarrassed as I tried to explain that a behavioural process seemed able to alleviate the debilitating physical symptoms that had blighted my life for so long. I didn't want to give credence to the misconception of CFS as a malingering set of vague symptoms rather than a real condition.

They were confused: "So it's a mental illness then and you're creating the symptoms?"; "maybe you'd just be getting better anyway, this therapy thing is probably giving you a confidence boost to do more without worrying about the repercussions", and "if it's an emotional anxiety thing, can't you just take a stronger antidepressant and try and relax a bit more".

Often, with great irony, when I attempted to explain the therapy that was helping me feel better my frustration about how this information was being received triggered more CFS symptoms. It was tricky getting people to accept that CFS is a physiological illness that involves complex interaction between multiple systems of the body, of which mental functioning is just one. I couldn't just magically switch off the symptoms by intellectually deciding to, or by following everyone's favourite advice and *trying* to relax a bit more.

How much easier it would have been if there was a diagnostic blood test for CFS that confirmed its existence as a legitimate medical condition. I wanted medication I could pop out of a blister pack and swallow with breakfast. Something that would miraculously fix my limbic response and alleviate each and every symptom without being a massive drag (and a huge expense) to implement like RT. An explanation and a treatment that people could get their heads around which would legitimise CFS once and for all.

Reverse therapy is not an exact science and it leaves questions unanswered: Why do some people have this sensitivity to limbic overactivity and others do not? And why had I got an acute onset of symptoms aged fifteen, yet not had a recurrence during my A-levels or when I did my degree which were stressful periods in my life with expectations running high? There were plenty of triggers for 'bodily distress' during the years that followed. Yet the symptoms had seemingly calmed down of their own accord at age sixteen after my O-levels, and had barely troubled me at all until I was twenty-eight when they resurfaced with full force.

I don't have the answers, and I'm still open to the possibility that a viral trigger, dysfunction of the cell mitochondria or some other factor, may also be involved. All I can say is that over the months that I began practising RT things began to change significantly. I needed a session every two to four weeks to identify what was working and what wasn't, and how to tweak things to remedy that, but I was getting the hang of it and it was life-changing.

15
Kicking the habit

Feeling well enough to get out and about again was exhilarating. I could walk further, use the Tube, go to the cinema, do my own shopping and carry it home. I remember grinning inanely at people on the Jubilee line just because I was on the Tube after a seven-year hiatus. The first time I entered Sainsbury's on my own to do the weekly shop it felt like a paradise. As I surveyed the aisles of fruit and veg and loaded up my trolley, I felt a surge of emotion and gratitude. A middle-aged woman noticed me welling up and assumed I was in distress: "Are you alright, luv? God, it's hell in here, isn't it. All these bloody people."

A few months later Sainsbury's was, infuriatingly, out of the fresh basil I needed for a recipe I was preparing; the instore Muzak was doing my head in and the herd of slow-moving shoppers was driving me to distraction. The simple joy I had felt on my first visit had been usurped by the irritating mundanity of everyday consumerism – I was back to 'normal'.

I took on a few pieces of freelance journalism, though I still couldn't spend too long on the computer without fatigue setting in. Work, deadlines and expectations was one of the areas I was finding tricky to crack with the RT. I felt a sense of needing to make up for lost time, to work hard to rebuild my career, to try and catch up with where I was supposed to be in life. But in other respects, I was improving in leaps and bounds – literally.

A friend had suggested I try a yoga class as a gentle way back into exercise. I went along, but soon realised I didn't really want to be there. The slow, reflective nature of yoga wasn't what I was craving, and the familiar fatigue and a dragging heaviness in my legs started up. These days I love yoga, but back then it just didn't feel right. I wasn't sure what I wanted to do to get moving again; I just knew it wasn't that.

On the bus home from the class a neon sign caught my eye with an arrow pointing down some steps to the basement: 'Kick boxing'. That sounded fun – I could kick, spin and fly through the air like Lara Croft. But after seven years of crushing fatigue and inactivity, how could I possibly build the fitness level required for kick boxing? It was madness. I had never been much good at sport and had always felt anxious about being pushed into gasping over-exertion by the sadistic school PE mistress. I should ease my way into some gentle exercise and not be an idiot.

While headmind continued to tell me what I should and shouldn't do, I got off the bus, followed the sign and went inside. Gary, the owner, was a former kick-boxing champion with a kick-arse attitude to match, but reassured me that I could go at my own pace if I wanted to give it a go. I went along to watch a session, loved it, and started a beginners class the following week.

The dojo had a padded floor so I felt confident enough to throw myself around, knowing that if I fell I'd 'bounce' back. I was so out of condition, my body hurt like hell for three days after the class, but this muscle soreness felt different to the heavy, dragging fatigue I had felt for years walking to the post box – and in the yoga class. I enjoyed the session so much and couldn't wait to go back. Over time the effects of being out of condition lessened and would disappear within a day or two.

I felt so alive in that dojo – happier than I had felt in years, my body and mind working in synergy. The sequences of moves we were learning flowed like a mantra – as my body moved, my mind was stilled. I was fully present in my body in a way I had perhaps never been. But if I started overthinking the practice or judged myself for getting a move wrong, my legs would immediately get that heavy, achy feeling; I'd suddenly be unable to flow through a sequence or, if we were 'light touch' sparring, I'd end up dazed on the floor – embarrassingly often tripping over myself rather than being caught off guard by my opponent.

It became clear that 'trying to get it right' in this context was going to have hard-hitting consequences. Yet, when I went with the flow and relied on instinct and muscle memory, I was not only capable but actually showed flare. When I was in the zone my moves and reflexes were lightning-fast and I could react to an opponent's move in a millisecond – perhaps there was an upside to having a hypervigilant limbic system after all. Exercise was at last generating energy rather than zapping it, and after decades of being 'allergic' to sport I was now in danger of becoming sporty.

Some of us in the class would go out for a drink afterwards. And Dean, the instructor who assisted Gary, provided an added incentive to keep training. He was ten years my junior and nothing like my usual type, but had the bluest eyes and a wry grin. He would get the train over from Hackney, bringing a selection of Hip Hop along with him that was always amped up on the gym's sound system before a class. He was a proper geezer, but had the inner calm and focus of a Zen monk.

One night, after a couple of whiskies, Dean let on that he'd done prison time in his late teens for armed robbery. He'd only been the getaway driver, though, and wasn't "carrying", which made it feel less of a big deal. Plus, he was keen to point out that he had read a whole library of books "including Charles Dickens" when he was banged up and had a different take on life now.

The reformed gangster thing gave him an edge. As he held up the kick pads and I slammed into them, breaking a sweat, there was a smouldering undercurrent of sexual tension. We had a snog a few months later at a Christmas party, but decided we were better off as sparring partners. Exercise just didn't get any better than this.

"You're a fighter, aren't you?"

My GP's words still echoed in my head from when I had gone to him aged fifteen with "post-viral fatigue".

Yes, I was a fighter, and now I had two belts and a couple of certificates to prove it. But instead of fighting my symptoms and pushing through them as he'd instructed, I was now listening to my body and acting on its wisdom. And in the space of a year, after numerous RT sessions, I was now fitter than I had been at any point in my adult life.

Years later I wrote an article about CFS for a health publication quoting several respected doctors in the field. The piece also included a couple of lines indicating that personally I had made progress using the RT approach. CFS hardliners were incensed that I was "claiming to have got better using bullshit quackery"; I was a "useless journalist peddling nonsense" and "a danger to people with ME who are seeking real answers".

Perhaps I should've expected the flack. After all, I had committed a cardinal sin in the ME community – I had got better and by controversial means. I knew how frustrating that was. In the midst of the illness I'd seen comments and social media posts from people evangelising about this and that – consuming large amounts of colloidal silver, the Lightning Process, Vega testing – the list was endless. If they'd got better, I had decided, it was because they didn't really have CFS in the first place – or not *my kind* of CFS. Perhaps they weren't affected that severely, their symptoms were primarily down to a mental health issue, or they were already recovering over time. It was the only way I could justify someone getting better from a treatment I had decided was nonsense – or worse, which I had blown money on but did nothing for me. Reverse therapy might well have been on my "bullshit quackery" list, had I not tried it and derived some benefit.

I certainly didn't find RT an easy fix. I have never evangelised about it, but rather attempted to explain its premise and the experience I had practising it. I'm aware that it doesn't work for everyone, and it doesn't always work for me these days; I'm open to other explanations of causes and mechanisms. A few years ago I was diagnosed with hypermobile Ehlers-Danlos syndrome and fibromyalgia which are also part of the picture when it comes to my chronic fatigue and vulval pain. Hypermobile Ehlers-Danlos syndrome is a connective tissue disorder which has undoubtedly influenced many of the symptoms and health issues I've had over the years. It causes generalised joint instability, chronic pain, fatigue and fragile, stretchy skin. A dysfunctional pelvic floor may also be a marker of the condition, resulting in problems with the musculature of the bladder and vagina. As I've got older, menopause and other age-related health issues have also entered the mix.

Eaton suggests that alongside CFS, conditions such as fibromyalgia and irritable bowel syndrome may also have the same cause – bodily distress syndrome. But it is important to note that RT cannot be applied to fatigue resulting from other physiological mechanisms e.g. wasting disease, chronic neuropathic pain, post-surgery fatigue and long Covid.

There is a reported overlap between CFS and fibromyalgia, bladder pain syndrome, hypermobility and vulvodynia. Of course, not everyone with one of these conditions will develop all of them, but scientific studies and anecdotal evidence indicates there is a correlation[12]. My gynaecologist often mentioned a subgroup of women attending her vulval clinic who presented symptoms of these other conditions as well as vulval pain.

I am not suggesting that vulvodynia might respond directly to RT in the same way my CFS symptoms appeared to. Vulvodynia is neuropathic pain that involves a complex interplay between muscles, nerves and the brain in a specific area of the body. Pelvic floor physiotherapy was by far the most successful treatment in that regard.

However, in my case, I can see a clear link between ongoing vulvodynia and chronic muscle tension experienced throughout my body, as the result of an overactive limbic system and bodily distress. Chronic muscle tension can occur in the pelvic floor, the gut, in the jaw and head, and neck and shoulders without us consciously realising it is happening (I recently scored highly on a diagnostic ADHD and hyperfocus questionnaire, which would also make sense as part of this picture).

In my teens, if my body had been in a state of bodily distress, that could have increased muscle tension in my pelvic floor which was exacerbated by the bout of thrush I had aged fifteen. The thrush symptoms could have been the trigger for a subconscious tightening of my vaginal muscles, as a protective response to the soreness and pain I was experiencing. The harsh topical antifungals I was prescribed long-term may also have aggravated my sensitive vulval skin.

Hypervigilance and constantly checking in on how my vulva was feeling would have set up a chronic pain loop between my brain and my pelvic floor, creating more muscle tension and aggravating the surrounding nerve endings. And that was the status quo for the next twenty years.

It was only when I began pelvic floor physio sessions that my vulval symptoms began to ease a little, but I still hadn't got over the final hurdle – having penetrative sex without pain. The final piece of the puzzle would show up, with the click of a mouse, at a bar in Shoreditch.

16

Cracked it

Ben had suggested the venue, but it was rammed with bankers and was only serving bar snacks, so we moved on to a quieter tapas joint. At forty-seven, he was twelve years older than me and outside the arbitrary age range I had set myself for online dating. But he looked in pretty good nick, assuming his profile pics were legit, so when he messaged me I made an exception.

I fancied him and the conversation flowed easily, even if he was rather more exuberant than I was used to. Ben was an actor, and it soon became clear that he was capable of projecting his voice to the back of any venue, regardless of whether or not it was a theatre. I squirmed behind my menu as he bellowed our order for tortilla and patatas bravas with the same vigour he might inject into a soliloquy at the Old Vic.

The chemistry was there in spades, though at times it was difficult to tell if we were having a sparky, sexually-charged conversation or just irritating each other; certainly, our views weren't always in sync. Still, I saw him a second time and as we got to know each other his openness and humour won me over. Plus, I would soon discover, he possessed the remarkable ability to remain totally unfazed in the face of vulval adversity. It became evident that I could share pretty much anything with Ben when it came to sex and vulval pain, and he would meet it with an energy and candour I hadn't encountered with previous partners.

Somehow, Ben hit upon the perfect balance of understanding and support whilst also gently nudging me forwards – in terms of managing the pain and believing recovery was possible. Rather than passively accepting non-penetrative sex as our only option (or me grinning and bearing a quick shag to pretend I was normal) he actively wanted to help us fix it. Instead of it being my issue, it became our project. Although that makes it sound like a dull work initiative when what we got up to was way more fun than that – once I'd got past the shock of our first fumble.

Oh crap, I thought, as we got down to it on his sofa. Remarkably, Ben's larger-than-life personality wasn't his biggest attribute. "Bigger is better" is hard-wired into our collective sexual psyche, but the prospect of a small to average encounter would've put a much bigger smile on my face. Even oral sex was a stretch until I got a bit handy.

(I'm hypermobile – double-jointed if you like – which means my joints are generally looser than they should be. I once yawned over-exuberantly upon waking and dislocated my jaw. After hyperventilating with shock for half an hour, I managed to relax enough to pull my jaw down and back into place with a crunch. It hurt like hell, and my mandibular joint was still smarting six months later. Now I yawn sideways and warm up my facial muscles before opening wide – for the dentist.)

Thankfully though, sex with Ben was more than the sum of our parts. It was fun, it was hot, and we laughed ourselves stupid – from his warehouse flat to his steamed-up Audi to the disabled toilet at the National Gallery. And we got creative – from props to toys to the contents of the freezer.

We moved between me being present with any uncomfortable sensations and relaxing around them (rather than tensing up) to techniques that would move my attention away from the focus of the pain; using plenty of hypoallergenic lube (no glycerin, no fragrance, no silicone) and clitoral stimulation during penetration helped shift my perception towards pleasure rather than discomfort. I found that exhaling and gently bearing down through my pelvic floor helped too.

Penetrative sex wasn't always the focus, but I felt comfortable with us nudging things in that direction. I was using the vaginal dilators at home, and doing the breathing and exercises my physiotherapist had prescribed to relax my overactive pelvic floor. Gradually, I was beginning to free up my chronically tight muscles and relax my nervous system's response to the 'pain loop'.

I discovered that filling one of my hollow plastic dilators with water and popping it in the freezer pimped it up from dull medical device to practical sex toy. Inserting a cold dilator temporarily numbed the pain a little. (Note: never put ice directly on the vulva or in the vagina – it can damage the sensitive mucosa, and cold therapy isn't for everyone.)

Sometimes, in my enthusiasm to move things forward, I'd overdo it and my nerve endings would be zinging with irritation for a couple of days. I'd have to wait until things calmed down and drop back to my base-line level of activity and edge forward more gently. It was frustrating, and often getting stressed about the situation amped up my pain level even further. But we were making progress, and eventually I got to the point where having Ben inside me was tolerable rather than painful. Incredibly, he would stay hard even if I asked him to stop moving. We'd exchange a bit of banter and I'd relax around any discomfort. Then we would carry on, or stop and switch to non-penetrative sex.

This erratic approach – and me declaring "I'm getting sore, we need to stop" – might understandably have given most men the flop. I did wonder if perhaps Ben was enhancing his staying power. Alice chose the red pill to visit Wonderland, but maybe he was popping a magic blue one to help us on our way. He wasn't, he said, and a surreptitious rummage in his bathroom cabinet failed to uncover a hidden stash of Viagra.

As an actor, perhaps he was just adept at staying 'in the zone'. Or maybe his background in executive coaching was coming into play; I got the feeling he was rather enjoying this role as transformational coach and sex guru. Or could it be that this mix of openness and trust combined with chemistry, humour and creativity was creating the perfect frisson for both of us? Whatever the reason, it was working.

This type of active 'facilitative' support was proven in one scientific study to be the best approach to managing vulvodynia and painful sex in a relationship: "Partner responses can be solicitous (attention and sympathy), negative (hostility and frustration), and facilitative (encouragement of adaptive coping)"[1]. Findings suggest that facilitative partner responses improve sexual functioning whereas solicitous and negative responses may be detrimental.

In parallel to nudging things forward with Ben, I was still under the care of the vulval clinic and women's health physiotherapist, and using steroid ointment to manage my LS. I was also taking oral fluconazole twice a month (and directly after penetrative sex) to keep any low-level thrush at bay. We were making progress, until we hit a potential roadblock three months in.

I had stated on my dating profile that ultimately I was looking for a long-term partner and to have kids. One evening, Ben put on his serious face. This didn't "feel long-term" to him, he said. He didn't really know why, it was just a feeling, and he thought he should put his cards on the table because he knew what I was looking for from a relationship. But that didn't mean he wanted to put a stop to the great sex we were having, he added, upbeat all of a sudden. He was enjoying this. It was up to me. I just needed to "manage my emotions" around it.

What?! I thought. You don't think this is long-term but you want to keep having sex with me. Why wasn't I a long-term prospect? How was I supposed to "manage my emotions" around it? And how could I stay in a relationship that wasn't going anywhere? I was thirty-six and my biological clock was ticking. Okay, I wasn't entirely sure about our long-term prospects either, but I wasn't ready to have that possibility quashed entirely.

I decided we would stop seeing each other, and over the next few weeks we both went on a string of futile internet dates. But I missed the journey we had been on together. We had almost arrived at a place where pain-free sex was ours to explore. Why give up now when I had come this far?

And so I called him. We wouldn't sleep with other people, that was the agreement. If either of us were to meet someone online and decide to pursue it we would tell the other first and call off our arrangement for a while.

This ought to have sent my anxiety levels sky-high, but to my surprise it felt strangely liberating – to begin with at least. I trusted him to be honest and open; I could express myself sexually without inhibition, knowing that nothing I asked for, or did, or couldn't do would upset our long-term prospects, because there weren't any.

Over several months my experience of penetrative sex shifted from painful to tolerable until, at last, it moved from comfortable to pleasurable. I remember a Saturday afternoon in mid-summer when the enormity of it hit me; when I realised I had finally arrived in the promised land:

I'm lying on Ben's bed, naked and draped in the sheet, listening to him singing in the kitchen below, making coffee. A cool breeze blows in from across the river, rustling the window blind, but beneath the sheet my body is still warm and molten.

In this room strewn with hopes, dreams, and dirty laundry, something remarkable has just happened. I've had sex – 'real' sex – the chandelier-swinging, bed-breaking stuff of legend. And for the first time in my thirty-six years, IT DIDN'T HURT. Apart from cracking my head on the headboard and some mild carpet burn.

'Real' PiV sex is the norm. It is happening around the world every second of every day – in houses and hotels, in mud huts, igloos and skyscrapers; in the back of Ford Escorts and limousines; perhaps even one mile high in the club-class toilet of a 747. And now it is happening here, in this bedroom, in SE16. I want to shout it from the rooftops, from this open window high up above the Thames. I am gloriously average, a 'real' woman at last, and the world is my oyster.

Ben brings the coffee upstairs. He is grinning from ear to ear with triumphant satisfaction – the Bear Grylls of SE16. A man who has achieved a feat that no other has ever managed

– an ecstatic pain-free shag with me.

The coffee goes cold and once again we are singing the Song of Songs, with a rocking bass line, from our mountain top south of the river. And afterwards, the hush. He is lost in afternoon slumber and I am left trying to make sense of this force of nature we have unleashed. For years I have pursued pain-free sex like a holy grail, but now I realise this is not the end of a journey but the beginning.

Sunlight dances across the sheets and his sleeping face. Along the river, the bells ring out from St Mary's, heralding my arrival in the land of milk and honey. On the pavement below, a scrum of grubby pigeons are fighting over half-eaten fish'n'chips, unaware I am up above – a phoenix ready to soar. For years I have been living in a shadow world, but now I am ascending with fire and light. I am a queen of the underworld, and I am risen.

A car pulls up in the parking bays below with the radio on. Before the driver cuts the engine, I catch a few bars of '90s pop classic, 'Stay' by Shakespears Sister. The video promo flashes through my head – a glittering, grinning Siobhan Fahey makes her entrance halfway through like a gothic goddess; 'death' warmed up to a sizzle. Smiling, I imagine donning her sequins and smoky eyeliner and taking on the world. Up here above the Thames I could sail a thousand ships.

It felt wild, being able to move as one with a lover – fulfilling my potential, becoming who I was meant to be. Free of pain, I was able to relax enough to reach orgasm with Ben inside me – the first time that had been possible with a partner. Le petit mort: that's how orgasm used to be referred to by the French – 'a little death', alluding to a temporary loss of consciousness. If orgasm was 'a little death' then, to use a modern colloquialism, I was killing it big time.

There was the intense physical pleasure I was now experiencing after so many years of pain; the boost to my self-esteem – at last I was 'good enough' and a 'real' woman; and the emotional intensity of trusting a partner with my vulnerability so we could make this journey together. Often, when penetrative sex with previous partners had been painful, I'd had to get it over with swiftly, or mentally remove myself from the experience in order to detach from the discomfort. Now, I was fully present to sex, to life, to everything. The roadblocks of CFS and painful sex had been cleared from my path and the world was alive with possibilities.

Other emotions, though, had also begun to turn up in the wake of this shift – emotions that I had not been prepared for. Along with joy and hope came anger and sadness for what I had missed out on all these years, and a grinding determination to make up for lost time. And as I continued to explore these new depths of pleasure and connection with Ben, the great sex we were having had begun to blind me to the emotional consequences. Sex no longer hurt, but the nagging emotional discomfort I felt afterwards was beginning to sting.

We catch our breath after having sex and I go to the bathroom. I can hear Ben listening to a voicemail on speaker-phone from his ex-girlfriend – the one he loved who dumped him; the one who has an uncanny habit of calling while we're getting it on.

Another weekend, Ben asks to postpone our meet-up. He has a second date with Wendy who plays the French horn in the London Philharmonic. He hasn't kissed Wendy yet and doesn't know how he feels about her. But I know how I feel about her; I can cope with the vague concept that Ben is looking for someone else, but when the generalisation has a name it cuts like a sharp scratch. He reminds me that he listens to anecdotes about my dates – he just manages his emotions around it.

A few months on, Ben landed a part in the touring version of a popular West End musical. Two hours after an unusually lack-lustre shag, I watched him gyrating on stage in an orange glam-rock one-piece; the theatre clad with red velvet and gold trim; the audience on their feet, singing and cheering; the dopamine rush from this feel-good extravaganza a temporary painkiller for the growing emotional hurt I was feeling.

Our relationship was now more off than on, but it was easy to come back to what worked, and sex with Ben worked, even if the rest of the setup was becoming harder to manage. I had begun to feel this stifled sense of potential whenever we had sex, a creative energy that would build towards possibility, then die back. Rather than feeling invigorated after our encounters, when the endorphin rush diminished I felt deadened and sad. The death knoll had begun to sound for our not-so-long-term arrangement, but it would take a series of 'little deaths' to finally put it to sleep.

A few weeks later, the urge to feel him inside me again would be overwhelming, and I would justify the inevitable. Despite countless dates, there was no-one else on the horizon. And hadn't my gynaecologist told me to "use it or lose it" to maintain my level of sexual functioning? My sex drive was through the roof and after all the years of pain, wasn't I entitled to make up for all the great sex I had missed? I just needed to keep on managing my emotions as Ben was doing. The emotional pain would be numbed by the novocaine of desire.

Along with these justifications, a powerful biological longing was kicking in. Mid-month I was becoming more acutely aware of the musky scent of ovulation; sometimes I'd even feel the nagging twinge of an ovary as it released another egg and chastised me yet again for scrambling the opportunity.

Around six months after I'd met Ben, the condom he was wearing had come off inside me. (We had been using condoms as our primary form of birth control.) Poking around to retrieve it gave me a horrible bout of cystitis and the biggest flare up of vulval pain I'd had in months. It was compounded by the hormonal surge of the morning-after pill, which we had decided I would take as I was mid-cycle and most likely ovulating. It dispelled any concerns about a pregnancy complicating our arrangement, but kicked off a thrush infection and a cycle of pain that went on for several weeks.

Almost three years later, after I had just turned thirty-eight, I was mid-cycle again and the urge to do what my biology demanded was palpable. I found myself staring at a spent condom in my bedside wastepaper basket. While Ben was in the bathroom, a thought flashed through my mind – I could retrieve it, turn it inside out, and send his sperm on a date with destiny.

I felt a flicker of excitement. But it was soon followed by the reality check of what that might actually mean in practical terms. If I were to get pregnant by stealth, I would be making a huge life choice on Ben's behalf without his consent and entangling us for a lifetime. I had very little money; I was still doing part-time freelance work and trying to escape the welfare system, and Ben was deep in debt. Outside of the sex we kept returning to, we were jarring on each other and the "manage your emotions" coaching speak was getting old. I was still holding out for happy ever after – 2.5 kids and a scruffy dog with my ever-elusive soulmate.

As I stared into the bin, I suddenly realised the pitfalls were outweighing the payoffs. I could see what it was and what it wasn't. I could no longer manage my feelings around what we were doing – I no longer wanted to. It was draining me of energy and self-esteem. Yes, I could now have pleasurable pain-free sex, but I needed a relationship that didn't hurt emotionally. I needed to move on and stop heading backwards between internet dalliances.

But this journey with Ben had been a remarkable ride. We had developed an intimacy, a trust and connection that survived – for a while at least – outside the bounds of the committed relationships we were both seeking.

And Mamma Mia, the image of him on stage in those sequinned satin flares still plays like a hologram whenever I hear an ABBA track. He's not a family man, or a football fan, and his name's not Harry, but I will always remember 'Our Last Summer', and that hot July day in SE16 when I spread my wings and soared above the Thames.

Epilogue

Thirty years ago – sitting nervously in GUM clinic waiting rooms – I considered 'real' sex to be PiV penetration, something I couldn't manage without searing pain. If the parts that made me physically female didn't function properly, was I a 'real' woman? It was a question that cut to the core of my identity and self-worth. I longed to feel 'normal' – to feel gloriously average.

But how do we decide what's 'normal' and what's 'real'? Is 'normal' about conforming to a prescribed standard – a PiV benchmark that's typical, usual and average? Today, 'real' sex means something different. It means an authentic sexual experience that's honest and genuine, and I get to decide those parameters with my partner.

Life's twists and turns continue to lead me off the straight and narrow. At times the vulval pain has returned with a vengeance and with it the familiar feelings of frustration and lack, but I've also enjoyed lengthy periods of joyous respite. I used to view life's erratic states of being as clear and contrasting opposites – feeling happy or sad, pain or pleasure, chronically ill or permanently cured. Over the years, I have learnt to navigate the space in between.

As I write this, the Paris Olympics are underway and I am watching Britain's top athletes undertaking incredible feats of strength and endurance. They are inspirational – a testament to years of hard work and determination. But I'm also in awe of the many remarkable people I know whose courage and resilience goes unrecognised. The feats of endurance that happen in the shadows, in the mundane, in facing another day of chronic illness, pain and uncertainty.

Around the world, millions of women wake up daily to pain and suffering, facing desperate circumstances. Pleasurable, pain-free sex should be a basic human right along with access to essential women's health services. Speaking the truth of our sexual and reproductive experiences should be something all women feel comfortable sharing without fear of violence, reprisals or shame. So let's fire up our cauldrons and stir things up. Together we can make a difference and bring about real change for women worldwide. There are ways to get in touch and to get involved in the Resources section.

When I was nineteen, pain-free PiV was the holy grail – the elusive missing component to a happy and fulfilling life. But at thirty-six, riding high at last, I realised it was not the end of a journey, but the beginning of one. What I was actually searching for was real intimacy – physical and emotional. And that may or may not involve PiV; it's certainly not dependent upon it. These days, getting real means speaking up about what I've been through and feeling empowered by what it's taken to get here. It means being true to myself and authentic in my relationships.

Just as physical intimacy has been painful, so too has emotional intimacy. I've had to break open to experience the love I longed for. This journey is not a forever upward trajectory; it is still a rollercoaster ride twenty years on and I still count myself as a member of The 'Chilli Pepper Sex' club. But that's another story, one that would take me out of London to a rural meditation retreat where I spent three unexpected years of reflection; then down to the coast for a new life by the sea – a life of chance adventures, sexual highs and lows, of love and loss. I would also continue to live the question of children – of birth and rebirth – through to menopause and beyond. But for now, I pause this journey at thirty-six, draped in a sheet, on top of the world above the Thames – a phoenix rising. Whatever life throws at you, when you're feeling the burn, may you rise too.

Hidden voices

If you count yourself a member of the 'Chilli Pepper Sex' club you'll have your own unique experience of vulval pain. Though I hope that within these pages I have managed to highlight some shared aspects of living with the condition which many women will resonate with.

This is ostensibly a memoir and focusing on my personal experiences has felt like an authentic way to roll. As a cis white woman, I have slept primarily with men, though if I had to stick a label on my sexual identity, I'd probably opt for 'heteroflexible'; I've heard the term bandied about and it appears to be a 21st century term for 'a bit bi'. I had a crush on a girl in my French class at school, had a late attempt at a bi-curious phase in my mid-forties, and I've indulged my 'Shane' fantasy during multiple seasons of *The L-Word*. However, none of this I feel particularly qualifies me to speak about vulval pain and sexual health from a queer perspective. Nor do I have personal experience of living with these issues in the context of a different ethnicity, culture or gender identity.

The scope of this memoir does not allow for a deep dive into the personal experiences of others, but it feels important to include a few diverse voices here as an adjunct to my own. I have encountered some remarkable people over the years who have shared their stories with me, and their perspectives illuminate the varied landscape of vulval pain. They are all members of a global 'Chilli Pepper Sex' club. So, as I conclude my own story, I'll share some of their words. Names and other identifying details have been changed for anonymity unless stated otherwise.

'Dana'

Dana is a young woman living in the US who identifies as lesbian. She has been diagnosed with vulvodynia.

"A big obstacle in my vulvodynia journey has been invalidation by physical therapists (PTs) and homophobia from doctors. Being a lesbian already makes me feel 'different' or not a 'normal' woman who has 'normal' sex, and vulvodynia has compounded that.

Frequently gynaecologists, even pelvic pain doctors, are very focused on penetration by a penis – this led to a huge delay in my initial diagnosis, because I wasn't having 'pain with penetrative sex'. (I know many lesbians do have penetrative sex, and now I do as well with toys; but at the time I just had no interest and so didn't know if it would lead to pain.)

Doctors and PTs would focus solely on the size of object I could insert in my vagina, and not on how my muscles were feeling throughout the day, or on my generalised symptoms on my external vulva, or on how oral sex felt. (Yes, this isn't exclusively about being gay, but our heterocentric culture I think prioritises penetration generally.)

One doctor had zero interest in treating me until I pretended to maybe be interested in men. *Then* she finally wrote me a script. Because of course what matters is a man being pleasured! Even a hypothetical one! It's worrying when I don't know if a doctor is homophobic and might give me not as good treatment. I've also struggled to fill out questionnaires in doctors' offices and to talk to nurses who assume I need to be on some form of birth control to prevent pregnancy and are alarmed I'm not and that my partner doesn't have a penis. I've also felt uncomfortable with doctors using the phrasing of 'when did you lose your virginity?' as I don't really relate to the concept of virginity, but didn't want to come out and explain everything. When I did explain queer sex to a doctor it was more funny than anything else lol, but also 'bruh, why don't you know more about this at this point in your career?!'"

Unfortunately, Dana's experiences of sexual healthcare are not uncommon and although clinicians are becoming more clued up these days in their approach to sexual orientation and gender, more education is needed. However, there is some encouraging news about queer sexual health from a 2022 research study of dyspareunia (painful sex)[1]. Queer experiences and communities were "found to be associated with advantages in pain management, such as well-developed sexual communication skills, anatomic similarity to their partner, access to non-heteronormative sexual scripts and a focus on nurturing desire".

'Duncan'

Duncan is a white heterosexual man in his early forties living in the UK. He has been in a relationship with Aisha, who is from a mixed ethnic background, for two years. Aisha was diagnosed with provoked vulvodynia a year ago which started after a severe urinary tract infection.

"If I'm honest, I do miss penetrative sex. I know Aisha misses it too and I know she's doing everything she can to try and fix the issue and I respect that. The way I see it, I could have a health problem at some point that might be hard for us to cope with and I know she would support me no matter what. We still do other stuff like oral sex and use sex toys and I've realised that what I want is to be having sex with her, not someone else, even if that means having our version of sex that is different to what people think of as 'normal'. At times it has done my head in a bit because I've felt bad about wanting penetrative sex and about missing it and about causing her pain when we've tried it. To begin with I also thought 'maybe it's me' and maybe she'd gone off me and that was why [she was experiencing painful sex]. Sometimes I'd lose my erection because I was worried about hurting her.

It's sometimes tough for both of us to talk about and to be honest about it all, but it's not a deal breaker. We managed to get a few sessions of couples therapy which helped, as well as us having individual counselling. I'd say to other partners out there, think about the rest of the time you're spending with your partner. If you're compatible, you love spending time together, and the relationship is mostly great, then sex is a part of it, not all of it. And there are other ways of having sex that can be fun if you experiment together. I can't pretend sex isn't important to me, but for me being with the right person is more important long term and you can work on the sex side of things together. There's no-one I'd rather do life with than Aisha, and I know that because I've had quite a few relationships. So, with the vulvodynia we just take it one day at a time and deal with it together."

A research study published in 2023, which explored men's experiences of their partner's female sexual pain, confirms that much of what Duncan is feeling is a common experience[2]. Some participants expressed concern that their partners' pain might be the result of a lack of attraction towards them, and others spoke about feelings of shame that their own sexual desire was still present. Several indicated that although they had no issue with not having penetrative sex, their partners found this hard to believe given that PiV is a social norm.

The prevalence of provoked vulvodynia has been reported to be lower in black compared to white and Latina women[3]. It has been suggested that cultural influences and different underlying pain mechanisms may contribute to differences in symptom reporting by race. For example, one study found that white women were more likely to refer to their vulval pain as burning or stinging (key markers for a diagnosis of provoked vulvodynia) whereas black women more often described their pain as aching[4].

Irina and Anastasia

Irina and Anastasia are young women in their twenties living in Russia. They both had vulvodynia for several years but are now managing their pain successfully. They have chosen to use their real names and to include their contact details as they want to encourage a global dialogue about how best to treat vulvodynia. They employed an interpreter to translate their comments into English and their transcript has been edited further for coherence and length. They have asked that their Instagram IDs be included: @vulvodynia.help (Irina) and @vulvodynia_rus (Anastasia).

In a world where countries and cultures continue to clash, and war and violence is ever present, it feels more important than ever to see the humanity in other people and to connect as individuals. If vulvodynia can help us recognise that as women we all share the same pain and the same emotions regardless of our geography and beliefs, that can only be a good thing. And if it results in a sharing of global resources to successfully treat vulval pain, better still.

Anastasia

"My name is Anastasia Kaminskaya and I had several years of chronic vulval pain so I know all the features of this condition from personal experience. I started a microblog about living with vulvodynia and shared whatever information I could find for other Russian women. I've been free of vulval pain for more than two years and as a practising psychologist I now work with Irina to try and help other women with vulvodynia. By analysing dozens of letters from girls all over Russia, Irina and I were able to understand the specifics of vulvodynia treatment in our country from different angles.

The main problem of vulvodynia treatment in Russia is the low awareness in the medical community of pelvic floor neuropathy and sexual dysfunction. This results in a long time to get the correct diagnosis (five to seven years on average) and wrong treatments which often leads to an aggravation of the condition. However, more and more doctors are studying the pelvic dysfunction topic in Russia, and Irina and I have shared the methods with them that helped us recover so we hope to help more women.

Before a correct diagnosis is made, a woman might try everything from antibiotics to surgery with no positive effect. Even a correct diagnosis of vulvodynia does not mean recovery as the condition is considered incurable by the medical community here. Therefore, after learning the diagnosis, a woman is left alone with her pain. At this point, we believe the right psychological attitude is key, as Irina will explain."

Irina

"My name is Irina Popova and for me the pain of vulvodynia was terrible and unbearable. You'll always remember the moment when pain came into your life – it literally knocks you down. That's what happened to us girls from Russia. Anastasia and I lived a thousand kilometres away from each other, but we had similar experiences. My region is located in the heart of Russia and Anastasia's home is in the east. Like most of the girls with vulvodynia we have connected with in Russia, we underwent treatment in Moscow which is in the western part of our country.

It took me six years to get the correct diagnosis and over those years I tried at least six types of treatment in three Russian cities. I was all alone with my problem. The treatments didn't work so instead, from the neurophysiological side, I began to look at the connection between anxiety and pain and this approach is what helped me personally. I am now a master's student in neurophysiology at Moscow State University and I am striving to consolidate my findings concerning vulvodynia in science.

Based on my research and work experience with Anastasia, we noticed that many women with vulvodynia (including ourselves) are overly anxious people. This personality type was there prior to the vulvodynia and the desire to 'heal at any cost' is especially strong.

Increased attention to body sensations, anxiety and disappointment from failed healing attempts creates a vicious circle of pain. To heal, I stopped seeing my own body as the enemy and fighting against it. I needed deep psychological and physical relaxation because my struggle against the symptoms was multiplying the muscle tension and increasing the pain. This is what our professional approach to treating vulvodynia is now based on. My wish is that we can solve the problem of vulvodynia not through struggle and suffering, but rather being explorers of our own bodies, thoughts and lives. Pain may sometimes be a 'notification' from your body asking for more attention, love and care."

Irina's and Anastasia's experiences and approach mirror findings from researchers in other countries. A US study published in 2011 found that "DSM-IV-diagnosed mood and anxiety may influence the development of unexplained vulvar pain" and established that ongoing vulvodynia symptoms may lead to a new or recurrent mood or anxiety disorder[5]. Certainly, there appears to be a cohort of women with vulvodynia who have a pre-existing tendency for anxiety, perfectionism and hyperfocus, and I count myself in this category.

Another study, published by Canadian researchers in 2020, demonstrated that mindfulness-based cognitive behavioural therapy was effective in improving symptoms in women with provoked vulvodynia[6]. Clearly, therapeutic practices that calm the autonomic nervous system are useful in treating some women with vulvodynia. However, it is important to remember that multiple factors may be involved in perpetuating vulval pain, often leading to the development of a vulval pain syndrome, which is unique to the individual. Nerves, muscles, hormones, inflammation and dermatological factors may all play a part in chronic vulval pain.

'Annie'

Annie is ninety-four and lives in the UK. Her feelings of shame about her sexual health issue in the early 1960s almost prevented her from having children. Annie's experience highlights the stigma that has long inhabited women's sexual health.

"After Frank and I got married we wanted to have a family straight away as we were getting on a bit. I was thirty, which was late to marry back then, and Frank was in his early forties. All these years later it still feels upsetting. Until now, I haven't spoken to anyone about what happened apart from Frank and my mother, as back then we just didn't share that sort of thing. It was private and you just got on with it as best you could.

We had been married for six years and still hadn't had children. When our families and friends enquired we just told them we were having difficulties conceiving and left it at that. The truth was that we couldn't have children because we couldn't have sexual intercourse. Even now, after all this time, I can still feel the shame and embarrassment of it.

I was a virgin when we married, and when we tried to have intercourse there seemed to be a physical block in the way and it was painful. I didn't want to see a doctor as I was too embarrassed. I was also frightened about what they might tell me – I didn't want to find out that I wasn't like other women and that I wasn't normal. I thought it was just how my body was and that I'd have to live with it. I was so upset and that upset Frank. He was so kind and said he loved me and that it was okay and we didn't have to keep trying to have intercourse if it was difficult. It was our problem and our secret – I think we both blamed ourselves as Frank thought he was doing something wrong and I thought it was my fault. We tried to just get on with things and not think about it too much.

After several years, we decided we would start on the adoption process to have a family that way. But then we received the news that we couldn't adopt because Frank was considered too old. We were devastated and I remember Frank suddenly leapt up and rushed out of the house. He said, 'I'm going for a walk, I'll be back later.' I just sat there and cried.

When he got home he put his arms around me and said, 'It's going to be alright. I managed to see the new doctor at the surgery and she's sending us to see a consultant in London.' I felt nervous about it but I knew it might be our only hope to try and have children. The gynaecologist examined me and said, 'You're so narrow you couldn't even get a pencil in there.' He said I would need a vaginal widening operation and that after that we would be able to have intercourse and to have children. I didn't ask what exactly was wrong with me or what the operation would involve, I just wanted it over with as soon as possible. Back then you didn't ask questions – you just followed the doctor's advice.

I spent a week in hospital recovering from the operation. When I woke up after the anaesthetic I was stuffed with wadding down there. When the doctor pulled it out [of my vagina] he wasn't very gentle and it was like having my insides pulled out. It was a horrible and humiliating experience which they hadn't prepared me for at all, but thankfully the operation was a success.

After I had recovered the consultant laughed and said that now I was wide enough to give birth to an elephant. I had to use vaginal dilators – glass things, I've still got them – that were different sizes, to keep things stretched.

Frank and I were able to have intercourse at last and we couldn't quite believe it but I was pregnant within six months. We were just overjoyed, so happy. I gave birth to Christopher nine months later – he was 8lbs 6oz.

I still have the dilators, you know, in their cardboard box in the back of the wardrobe. I know it sounds silly but I have never been able to throw them out. I think I was worried that someone might find them in the rubbish. I suppose I hid them away along with my memories about it all."

I had known Annie for years before she felt comfortable telling me her story. When I mentioned I was writing a book about my experience of vulval pain she began to share her experience, in fragments. Then she asked if I might do her a small favour. She still didn't know how to get rid of the dilators, she said, but she would like them gone now.

I took the cardboard box home with me. There were four of them in various sizes, made of hollow glass like pointy-ended chemistry test tubes. Inserting hollowed glass into the vagina seemed to me a rather risky business. Clearly the bar for gynae health and safety wasn't as high in the 1960s, although inserting today's phalate-infused plastic and rubber products carries its own health risks.

I took them to the local tip, along with some other items I had for recycling. As I posted them one by one through the slot at the bottle bank, I hoped that Annie would now be free of the shame and upset she had associated with them.

At first, I wondered if Annie may have had vaginismus – a common condition in which the muscles of the vagina tighten involuntarily during attempted penetration. She had told me that when she was a teenager in the 1940s, her mother had made it clear on multiple occasions that getting pregnant out of wedlock was the worst thing she could ever do. Annie said that during her teens she noticed that she consciously "tightened up down there" whenever sex was referred to.

A rare congenital condition called Mayer-Rokitansky-Küster-Hauser (MRKH) syndrome can also be the cause of a narrow vagina. Girls with MRKH are born with an underdeveloped or absent vagina and uterus. They may however have normal female genitalia and female chromosomes. Lack of menstruation during puberty is often the first sign that there is an issue. As Annie had periods and a functioning uterus, it seems unlikely MRKH was the cause.

Another possibility is that Annie had a congenital abnormality of the hymen. The condition is estimated to affect 1 in 2,000 women and can make vaginal penetration difficult or impossible[7]. (The hymen is a thin mucous membrane that partially covers the opening to the vagina, until it is either torn or stretched. It is usually a crescent moon-shaped fringe of tissue, but can vary in shape, size, thickness and elasticity.) It is possible that Annie had a microperforate or septate hymen. A microperforate hymen has a very small opening that allows menstrual blood to flow through, but may cause difficulties when inserting and / or removing tampons. A septate hymen means the entrance to the vagina has two small holes with a thin band of tissue running through the middle. Other hymenal variations may seal the vagina entirely, or hymenal tissue may form a ring around the vaginal entrance, or there may be several tiny holes rather than one[8]. Today, hymenal abnormalities are usually resolved by a minor surgical procedure known as a hymenectomy.

....

The stories I have included in this chapter explore vulval pain from various perspectives, but are by no means intended as a comprehensive overview. I am aware that genital pain affects a broad spectrum of people, many of whom are not represented here, including members of the trans community, and women who have experienced FGM. Having reached out to these communities, I appreciate the complex and sensitive nature of these experiences, and understand that cultural and clinical insight is necessary alongside varied personal experiences to provide context and clarity. Although there is not scope within this memoir to explore these issues in full, I hope that members of these communities will continue to make their voices heard through their own outreach.

It is a privilege to have been trusted with these powerful personal stories and I extend my thanks to those who have generously allowed me to include their perspectives here.

Acknowledgements

Many extraordinary people have travelled with me on my journey through vulval pain, associated health issues and the writing of this book.

An enormous thank you to all the women I have connected with over the years via the Vulval Pain Society (VPS), the London Vulval Pain Support Group and global online communities. You continue to be an inspiration, and I wish you well on your own journeys towards healing and recovery.

Thanks also to the remarkable Dr David Nunns, consultant gynaecologist, and founder and trustee of the VPS, who has worked tirelessly to achieve better care for women with vulval pain. I am also grateful to Professor Wendy Reid, my vulval specialist for many years until her well-deserved retirement from clinical practice. Her expertise, compassion and willingness to innovate were invaluable in managing my vulval pain.

To those closest to me, I also extend my appreciation: my good friend and creative collaborator Sabine Tyrvainen; my family – including Julian, who's had to hear more about my sexual health than any brother ever should; and to James who's been my partner in love, life and vulval flare-ups.

And finally, my gratitude goes out to my mother, my grandmothers and the generations of women before them whose myriad sexual and reproductive experiences birthed my own. I am here because of what you lived through.

Thank you.

Resources

Sally Turner
sallyjturner.com
Visit my online hub and find out more about my work in the women's health sector. If you'd like to drop me a line regarding this book, my podcast or other projects, I'd love to hear from you. Please get in touch via my website. You'll also find me on Instagram, X and Bluesky Social:
X: @sallyjaneturner
Instagram: @sally_jane_turner
Bluesky Social: @sallyjaneturner.bsky.social

Women4Real: Getting real about women's sexual health
sallyjturner.com/podcast
Join me as I talk to expert clinicians, scientists and researchers, and women living with sexual health issues. Together, we'll bust misconceptions and bring you the facts and the latest thinking on everything from chronic thrush, hymens and herpes to labiaplasty and vulvodynia. Available on all major podcast platforms.

The Vulval Pain Society
vulvalpainsociety.org
The go-to UK resource for anyone seeking advice and support for vulval pain. You'll find the latest information here on vulvodynia and links to resources for other vulval conditions such as lichen sclerosus and pudendal nerve entrapment.

Webchat forums
Online chat forums such as Facebook and Reddit host discussion threads about women's sexual health on topics including vulvodynia, lichen sclerosus and more. Great for mutual support, but proceed with caution if treatment advice is given, and ignore the doom mongers.

Notes

2 – Molten underworld

1. Wiertsema, S. P., van Bergenhenegouwen, J., Garssen, J. and Knippels, L. M. J. (2021) 'The Interplay between the Gut Microbiome and the Immune System in the Context of Infectious Diseases throughout Life and the Role of Nutrition in Optimizing Treatment Strategies', *Nutrients*. 13(3):886. doi: 10.3390/nu13030886. PMID: 33803407; PMCID: PMC8001875.
2. Kumar, A., Pramanik, J., Goyal, N., Chauhan, D., Sivamaruthi, B. S., Prajapati, B. G. and Chaiyasut, C. (2023) Gut Microbiota in Anxiety and Depression: Unveiling the Relationships and Management Options. *Pharmaceuticals* (Basel). 16(4):565. doi: 10.3390/ph16040565. PMID: 37111321; PMCID: PMC10146621.
3. Nie, S., Ge, Y. (2023) 'The link between the gut microbiome, inflammation, and Parkinson's disease', *Appl Microbiol Biotechnol*. 107(22):6737-6749. doi: 10.1007/s00253-023-12789-6. PMID: 37736791.
4. W. E. Anthony et al. (2022) 'Acute and persistent effects of commonly used antibiotics on the gut microbiome and resistome in healthy adults', *Cell Rep.*, vol. 39, no. 2, p. 110649. doi: 10.1016/j.celrep.2022.110649.
5. Foxman, B., Muraglia, R., Dietz, J. et al. (2013) 'Prevalence of recurrent vulvovaginal candidiasis in 5 European countries and the United States: results from an internet panel survey', *Journal of lower genital tract disease*. 17(3), 340-345.

3 – Poker face

1. Turner, S., Patient, Oral sex: what you need to know to stay healthy. Retrieved 9/10/24 from https://patient.info/news-and-features/can-you-catch-hiv-chlamydia-from-oral-sex.
2. Ibid.

3. Vulval Pain Society. Retrieved 9/10/24 from https://vulvalpainsociety.org/about-vulval-pain/vulval-pain-conditions/vulvodynia/.

4 – A Frank encounter

1. Rosen, A. D., Rosen T. (1999) 'Study of condom integrity after brief exposure to over-the-counter vaginal preparations', *South Med J*. 92(3):305-7. doi: 10.1097/00007611-199903000-00009. PMID: 10094272.
2. Terence Higgins Trust. Retrieved 9/10/24 from https://www.tht.org.uk/sexual-health/improving-your-sexual-health/contraception/emergency.
3. Ibid.
4. National Cancer Institute. Retrieved 9/10/24 from https://www.cancer.gov/about-cancer/causes-prevention/risk/infectious-agents/hpv-and-cancer
5. U.S. Centers for Disease Control and Infection. Retrieved 9/10/24 from https://www.cdc.gov/hpv/vaccines/reasons-to-get.html?CDC_AAref_Val=https://www.cdc.gov/hpv/parents/vaccine/six-reasons.html
6. Ibid.
7. Okunade, K. S. (2020) 'Human papillomavirus and cervical cancer', *J Obstet Gynaecol*. 40(5):602-608. doi: 10.1080/01443615.2019.1634030. Epub 2019 Sep 10. Erratum in: *J Obstet Gynaecol*. 2020 May;40(4):590. doi: 10.1080/01443615.2020.1713592. PMID: 31500479; PMCID: PMC7062568.
8. Cancer Research UK. Retrieved 11/10/24 from https://www.cancerresearchuk.org/about-cancer/cervical-cancer/risks-causes
9. Nguyen, N. P., Nguyen, L. M., Thomas, S., Hong-Ly, B., Chi, A., Vos, P., Karlsson, U. and Vinh-Hung, V. (2016) 'International Geriatric Radiation Oncology Group. Oral sex and oropharyngeal cancer: The role of the primary care physicians', *Medicine (Baltimore)*. 95(28):e4228. doi: 10.1097/MD.0000000000004228. PMID: 27428229; PMCID: PMC4956823.

10. UK Government Publications. Retrieved 11/10/24 from https://www.gov.uk/government/publications/hpv-vaccine-vaccination-guide-leaflet/information-on-the-hpv-vaccination-from-september-2023

6 – Scrounging and lounging

1. World Health Organization. Retrieved 11/10/24 from https://www.who.int/standards/classifications/frequently-asked-questions/chronic-fatigue-syndrome
2. Action for ME. Retrieved 11/10/24 from https://www.actionforme.org.uk/get-information/what-is-me/what-does-me-feel-like/
3. Ibid.
4. National Institute for Health and Care Excellence. Retrieved 11/10/24 from https://www.nice.org.uk/guidance/ng206

6 – Woo-Woo Street

1. *Daily Info*. Retrieved 16/10/24 from https://www.daily-info.co.uk/feature/2772/derek-acorah 2008
2. *The X Files: The Truth Is Out There*. Retrieved 16/10/24 from https://www.imdb.com/video/vi1053801753/
3. Jalāl al-Dīn Muḥammad Rūmī. Quotation rights granted by rumi.net

9 – Eve's volcano

1. *The Week*. Retrieved 16/10/24 from https://theweek.com/articles/459434/brief-history-what-happens-vegas-stays-vegas
2. Institoris, H., Sprenger, J. and Summers, M. (1948) *Malleus Maleficarum*, Pushkin Press.
3. Angier, N. ESSAY; In the History of Gynecology, a Surprising Chapter. *New York Times*, February 23, 1999, Archives. Retrieved 16/10/24 from https://www.nytimes.com/1999/02/23/science/essay-in-the-history-of-gynecology-a-surpr ising-chapter.html
4. Freud, S. (1905) *Drei Abhandlungen zur Sexualtheorie (Three Essays on the Theory of Sexuality)*, Leipzig und Wein, Franz Deuticke.

5. Pompeii Sites. Retrieved 16/10/24 from https://pompeiisites.org/en/pompeii-map/analysis/the-casts/

10 – The 'Chilli Pepper Sex' club

1. Sophia, E. *Women's Republic*. Retrieved 16/10/24 from https://www.womensrepublic.net/vagina-the-oppressive-original-meaning-and-why-it-matters-today/
2. Online Etymology Dictionary. Retrieved 16/10/24 from https://www.etymonline.com/word/vulva
3. Ibid.
4. McCartney, J. *The Great Wall of Vulva*. Retrieved 16/10/24 from https://www.thegreatwallofvulva.com/
5. Juggs, O. The unknown etymology of your least favourite word. *The Trail*. Retrieved 27/11/24 from https://trail.pugetsound.edu/?p=7686
6. Rosen, N. O., Bergeron, S., Sadikaj, G., Glowacka, M., Delisle, I. and Baxter, M. L. (2014) 'Impact of male partner responses on sexual function in women with vulvodynia and their partners: a dyadic daily experience study', *Health Psychology:* official journal of the Division of Health Psychology, American Psychological Association. 33. 10.1037/a0034550.
7. Turner, S. and Tyrvainen, *S. Painful Sex v. Normal Sex: the differences explained with food*, Women4Real. Retrieved 16/10/24 from https://www.sallyjturner.com/women4real

Chapter 11 – Long lost lips

1. Tran, D. A., Tan, X., Macri, C. J., Goldstein, A. T. and Fu, S. W. (2019) 'Lichen Sclerosus: An autoimmunopathogenic and genomic enigma with emerging genetic and immune targets', *Int J Biol Sci*. 15(7):1429-1439. doi: 10.7150/ijbs.34613. PMID: 31337973; PMCID: PMC6643151.
2. McCloud, K. Grand Designs, Boundless Productions, series 13, ep 5.
3. The Courts should keep out of our sex lives. *Spiked*. Retrieved on 29/1//24 from https://www.spiked-online.com/2011/09/01/the-courts-should-keep-out-of-our-sex-lives/#.WHjBcPmLTcs

4. Binning, C. Casual sex, STIs, and the criminal law. *Lexology*. Retrieved on 29/11/24 from https://www.lexology.com/library/detail.aspx?g=1f8f0941-1d7c-41f2-981c-e94d88e3ed8a

Chapter 12 – Houston, we have a problem

1. Fictional title as actual title not recalled.
2. World Metrics. Pornography statistics. Retrieved on 30 September 2024 from https://worldmetrics.org/pornography-statistics/
3. Wright, P. J., Tokunaga, R. and Kraus, A. (2015). 'A Meta-Analysis of Pornography Consumption and Actual Acts of Sexual Aggression in General Population Studies', *Journal of Communication*. 66. n/a-n/a. 10.1111/jcom.12201.
4. Wright, P. J., Tokunaga, R. and Herbenick, D. (2023). 'But Do Porn Sites Get More Traffic than TikTok, OpenAI, and Zoom?' *The Journal of Sex Research*, 60(6), 763–767. https://doi.org/10.1080/00224499.2023.2220690
5. *Adult Video News*, October 2000; "EroticBid.Com Now the Leader for Online Auctions", eroticbid.com Press Release, *Adult Industry News*, April 21, 2001.
6. "Houston: An Intimate Portrait". *New York Observer*. August 20, 2000.
7. Turner, S. "Labiaplasties – what are they and are they ever medically necessary?" patient.info. Retrieved on 29/22/24 from https://patient.info/news-and-features/labiaplasties-what-are-they-and-are-they-ever-medically-necessary
8. End FGM European Network. Retrieved on 30/11/24 from https://www.endfgm.eu/female-genital-mutilation/what-is-fgm/
9. Turner, S. "Myths about the hymen debunked." patient.info. Retrieved on 29/11/24 from https://patient.info/news-and-features/common-myths-about-the-hymen-debunked
10. World Health Organization. "United Nations agencies call for ban on virginity testing." Retrieved on 29/11/24 from https://www.who.int/news/item/17-10-2018-united-nations-agencies-call-for-ban-on-virginity-testing

11. "What was John Ruskin thinking on his unhappy wedding night?" The Guardian. Retrieved on 20/11/24 from https://www.theguardian.com/film/2010/mar/14/john-ruskin-wedding-effie-gray
12. "7 inspirational quotes from Kevin McCloud". Grand Designs magazine. Retrieved on 29/11/24 from https://www.granddesignsmagazine.com/kevin-mccloud/kevin-mccloud-quotes/

Chapter 13 – The floor keeps the score

1. Brotto, L. Bergeron, S. Zdaniuk, B. and Basson, R. (2020) 'Mindfulness and Cognitive Behavior Therapy for Provoked Vestibulodynia: Mediators of Treatment Outcome and Long-Term Effects', *Journal of Consulting and Clinical Psychology*. Vol. 88, No. 1, 48–64 ISSN: 0022-006X http://dx.doi.org/10.1037/ccp0000473
2. "When is *penetrate* a more appropriate choice than *pierce*?" miriam-webster.com. Retrieved on 30/11/24 from https://www.merriam-webster.com/thesaurus/pierce
3. Vocabulary.com. Retrieved on 30/11/24 from https://www.vocabulary.com/dictionary/penetration#
4. Stack Exchange. Retrieved on 30/11/24 from https://english.stackexchange.com/questions/142492/where-did-the-word-quim-come-from
5. Turner, S. "How to overcome vaginismus and relax your pelvic floor". patient.info. Retrieved on 30/11/24 from https://patient.info/news-and-features/how-to-overcome-vaginismus

Chapter 14 – One more try

1. reverse-therapy.com
2. Eaton, J. Reverse Therapy – Chronic Fatigue, Fibromyalgia and related disorders. Amazon. 2017, 2021.
3. Ibid.
4. Hoover, K. and Higginbotham K. Epstein-Barr Virus. [Updated 2023 Aug 8]. In: StatPearls [Internet]. Treasure Island (FL): StatPearls Publishing; 2024 Jan-. Available from: https://www.ncbi.nlm.nih.gov/books/NBK559285/
5. Luzuriaga, K. and Sullivan, J. (2010) 'Infectious mononucleosis', *New England Journal of Medicine*. 362(21):1993–2000

Chapter 15 – Kicking the habit

1. Maixner, W., Fillingim, R. B., Williams, D. A., Smith, S. B. and Slade, G. D. (2016) 'Overlapping Chronic Pain Conditions: Implications for Diagnosis and Classification', *J Pain*. 17(9 Suppl):T93-T107. doi: 10.1016/j.jpain.2016.06.002. PMID: 27586833; PMCID: PMC6193199.
2. Soogoor, A. and Narampanawe, B. (2024) 10 'Facts overlooking co-morbitities associated with vulvodynia', JMSMA Vol. 65, Issue 5/6. Retrieved on 30/11/24 from https://jmsma.scholasticahq.com/article/120331-10-facts-overlooking-co-morbitities-associated-with-vulvodynia

Chapter 16 – Cracked it

1. Rosen, N. O., Bergeron, S., Sadikaj, G., Glowacka, M., Delisle, I. and Baxter, M. L. (2014) 'Impact of male partner responses on sexual function in women with vulvodynia and their partners: a dyadic daily experience study', Health Psychology. 33(8):823-31. doi: 10.1037/a0034550. Epub 2013 Nov 18. PMID: 24245835.

Hidden voices

1. Ekholm, E., Lundberg, T., Carlsson, J., Norberg, J., Linton, S. J. and Flink, I. K. (2021). '"A lot to fall back on": experiences of dyspareunia among queer women', *Psychology & Sexuality*, 13(5), 1242–1255.
2. Lovell, D., Hayfield, N., and Thomas, Z. (2023). '"No one has ever asked me and I'm grateful that you have" men's experiences of their partner's female sexual pain', *Sexual and Relationship Therapy*, 1–24. https://doi.org/10.1080/14681994.2023.2293766
3. Brown, C. S., Foster, D. C., Bachour, C. C., Rawlinson, L. A., Wan, J. Y. and Bachmann, G. A. (2015) 'Presenting Symptoms Among Black and White Women with Provoked Vulvodynia', *J Womens Health* (Larchmt). 24(10):831-6. doi: 10.1089/jwh.2014.5164. Epub 2015 Aug 20. PMID: 26291682; PMCID: PMC4841081.
4. Ibid.
5. Khandker, M., Brady, S. S., Vitonis, A. F., Maclehose, R. F.,

Stewart, E. G. and Harlow, B. L. (2011) 'The influence of depression and anxiety on risk of adult onset vulvodynia', *J Women's Health* (Larchmt). 20(10):1445-51. doi: 10.1089/jwh.2010.2661. Epub 2011 Aug 8. PMID: 21823918; PMCID: PMC3186444.

6. Brotto, L., Bergeron, S., Zdaniuk and B., Basson, R. (2020) 'Mindfulness and Cognitive Behavior Therapy for Provoked Vestibulodynia: Mediators of Treatment Outcome and Long-Term Effects', *Journal of Consulting and Clinical Psychology*. Vol. 88, No. 1, 48 – 64 ISSN: 0022-006X http://dx.doi.org/10.1037/ccp0000473
7. Parazzini, F. and Cecchetti, G. (1990) 'The frequency of imperforate hymen in Northern Italy', *International Journal of Epidemiology,* Volume 19, Issue 3, Pages 763–764, https://doi.org/10.1093/ije/19.3.763
8. Turner, S. "Myths about the hymen debunked." patient.info. Retrieved on 29/11/24 from https://patient.info/news-and-features/common-myths-about-the-hymen-debunked

Printed in Dunstable, United Kingdom

65541319R00111